Allyn
and
Bacon

iSearch:
Psychology

Brian M. Kelly
Bridgewater College

Linda R. Barr
University of the Virgin Islands

Boston | New York | San Francisco
Mexico City | Montreal | Toronto | London | Madrid | Munich | Paris
Hong Kong | Singapore | Tokyo | Cape Town | Sydney

Contents

Introduction

Your professor assigns a research paper or group report that's due in two weeks—and you need to make sure you have up-to-date, credible information. Where do you begin? Today, the easiest answer is the Internet—because it can be so convenient and there is so much information out there. But therein lies part of the problem. How do you know if the information is reliable and from a trustworthy source?

iSearch: Psychology is designed to help you select and evaluate research from the Web to help you find the best and most credible information you can. Throughout this guide, you'll find:

- **A practical and to-the-point discussion of search engines.** Find out which search engines are likely to get you the information you want and how to phrase your searches for the most effective results.
- **Detailed information on evaluating online sources.** Locate credible information on the Web and get tips for thinking critically about websites.
- **Citation guidelines for Web resources.** Learn the proper citation guidelines for Web sites, email messages, listservs, and more.
- **Web activities for Psychology.** Explore the various ways you can use the Web in your courses through these online exercises.
- **Web links for Psychology.** Begin your Web research with the discipline-specific sources listed in this section. Also included is information about Web resources offered by Allyn & Bacon—these sites are designed to give you an extra boost in your Psychology courses.
- **A Quick Guide to ContentSelect.** All you need to know to get started with ContentSelect, a free research database that gives you immediate access to hundreds of scholarly journals and other popular publications, such as *Newsweek*.

So before running straight to your browser, take the time to read through this copy of *iSearch: Psychology* and use it as a reference for all of your Web research needs.

Conducting Online Research

Finding Sources:
Search Engines and Subject Directories

Your professor has just given you an assignment to give a five minute speech on the topic "gun control." After a (hopefully brief) panic attack, you begin to think of what type of information you need before you can write the speech. To provide an interesting introduction, you decide to involve your class by taking a straw poll of their views for and against gun control, and to follow this up by giving some statistics on how many Americans favor (and oppose) gun control legislation and then by outlining the arguments on both sides of the issue. If you already know the correct URL for an authoritative Web site like Gallup Opinion Polls (www.gallup.com) or other sites you are in great shape! However, what do you do when you don't have a clue as to which Web site would have information on your topic? In these cases, many, many people routinely (and mistakenly) go to Yahoo! and type in a single term (e.g., guns). This approach is sure to bring first a smile to your face when the results offer you 200,874 hits on your topic, but just as quickly make you grind your teeth in frustration when you start scrolling down the hit list and find sites that range from gun dealerships, to reviews of the video "Young Guns," to aging fan sites for "Guns and Roses."

Finding information on a specific topic on the Web is a challenge. The more intricate your research need, the more difficult it is to find the one or two Web sites among the billions that feature the information you want. This section is designed to help you to avoid frustration and to focus in on the right site for your research by using search engines, subject directories, and meta-sites.

Search Engines

Search engines (sometimes called search services) are becoming more numerous on the Web. Originally, they were designed to help users search the Web by topic. More recently, search engines have added features which enhance their usefulness, such as searching a particular part of the Web (e.g., only sites of educational institutions—dot.edu), retrieving just one site which the search engine touts as most relevant (like Ask Jeeves {www.aj.com}), or retrieving up to 10 sites which the search engine rank as most relevant (like Google {www.google.com}).

Search Engine Defined

According to Cohen (1999):

> "A search engine service provides a searchable database of Internet files collected by a computer program called a wanderer, crawler, robot, worm, or spider. Indexing is created from the collected files, and the results are presented in a schematic order. There are no selection criteria for the collection of files.
>
> A search service therefore consists of three components: (1) a spider, a program that traverses the Web from link to link, identifying and reading pages; (2) an index, a database containing a copy of each Web page gathered by the spider; and (3) a search engine mechanism, software that enables users to query the index and then returns results in a schematic order (p. 31)."

One problem students often have in their use of search engines is that they are deceptively easy to use. Like our example "guns," no matter what is typed into the handy box at the top, links to numerous Web sites appear instantaneously, lulling students into a false sense of security. Since so much was retrieved, surely SOME of it must be useful. WRONG! Many Web sites retrieved will be very light on substantive content, which is not what you need for most academic endeavors. Finding just the right Web site has been likened to finding diamonds in the desert.

As you can see by the definition above, one reason for this is that most search engines use indexes developed by machines. Therefore they are indexing terms not concepts. The search engine cannot tell the difference between the keyword "crack" to mean a split in the sidewalk and "crack" referring to crack cocaine. To use search engines properly takes some skill, and this chapter will provide tips to help you use search engines more effectively. First, however, let's look at the different types of search engines with examples:

TYPES OF SEARCH ENGINES		
TYPE	**DESCRIPTION**	**EXAMPLES**
1st Generation	• Non-evaluative, do not evaluate results in terms of content or authority. • Return results ranked by relevancy alone (number of times the term(s) entered appear, usually on the first paragraph or page of the site)	AltaVista (www.altavista.com/) Excite (www.excite.com) HotBot (www.HotBot.com) Infoseek (guide.infoseek.com) Ixquick Metasearch (ixquick.com) Lycos (www.lycos.com)
2nd Generation	• More creative in displaying results. • Results are ordered by characteristics such as: concept, document type, Web site, popularity, etc. rather than relevancy.	Ask Jeeves (www.aj.com/) Direct Hit (www.directhit.com/) Google! (www.google.com/) HotLinks (www.hotlinks.com/) Simplifind (www.simpli.com/) SurfWax (www.surfwax.com/) Also see Meta-Search engines below. EVALUATIVE SEARCH ENGINES About.Com (www.about.com) WebCrawler (www.webcrawler.com)
Commercial Portals	• Provide additional features such as: customized news, stock quotations, weather reports, shopping, etc. • They want to be used as a "one stop" Web guide. • They profit from prominent advertisements and fees charged to featured sites.	GONetwork (www.go.com/) Google Web Directory (directory.google.com/) LookSmart (www.looksmart.com/) My Starting Point (www.stpt.com/) Open Directory Project (dmoz.org/) NetNow (www.inetnow.com) Yahoo! (www.yahoo.com/)
Meta-Search Engines	Run searches on multiple search engines.	There are different types of meta-search engines. See the next 2 boxes.

(continued)

iSearch: Psychology

TYPES OF SEARCH ENGINES, *continued*		
TYPE	DESCRIPTION	EXAMPLES
Meta-Search Engines *Integrated Result*	• Display results for search engines in one list. • Duplicates are removed. • Only portions of results from each engine are returned.	Beaucoup.com (www.beaucoup.com/) Highway 61 (www.highway61.com) Cyber411(www.cyber411. com/) Mamma (www.mamma.com/) MetaCrawler (www. metacrawler.com/) Visisimo (www.vivisimo.com) Northern Light (www.nlsearch.com/) SurfWax (www.surfwax.com)
Meta-Search Engines *Non-Integrated Results*	• Comprehensive search. • Displays results from each search engine in separate results sets. • Duplicates remain. • You must sift through all the sites.	Dogpile (www.dogpile.com) Global Federated Search (jin.dis.vt.edu/fedsearch/) GoHip (www.gohip.com) Searchalot (www.searchalot.com) 1Blink (www.1blink.com) ProFusion (www. profusion.com/)

QUICK TIPS FOR MORE EFFECTIVE USE OF SEARCH ENGINES

1. Use a search engine:
   • When you have a narrow idea to search.
   • When you want to search the full text of countless Web pages
   • When you want to retrieve a large number of sites
   • When the features of the search engine (like searching particular parts of the Web) help with your search

2. Always use Boolean Operators to combine terms. Searching on a single term is a sure way to retrieve a very large number of Web pages, few, if any, of which are on target.
   • Always check search engine's HELP feature to see what symbols are used for the operators as these vary (e.g., some engines use the & or + symbol for AND).
   • Boolean Operators include:
     AND to narrow search and to make sure that **both** terms are included
       e.g:, children AND violence
     OR to broaden search and to make sure that **either** term is included
       e.g., child OR children OR juveniles
     NOT to **exclude** one term
       e.g., eclipse NOT lunar

iSearch: Psychology

3. Use appropriate symbols to indicate important terms and to indicate phrases (Best Bet for Constructing a Search According to Cohen (1999): Use a plus sign (+) in front of terms you want to retrieve: +solar +eclipse. Place a phrase in double quotation marks: "solar eclipse" Put together: "+solar eclipse" "+South America").

4. Use word stemming (a.k.a. truncation) to find all variations of a word (check search engine HELP for symbols).
   - If you want to retrieve child, child's, or children use child* (some engines use other symbols such as !, #, or $)
   - Some engines automatically search singular and plural terms, check HELP to see if yours does.

5. Since search engines only search a portion of the Web, use several search engines or a meta-search engine to extend your reach.

6. Remember search engines are generally mindless drones that do not evaluate. Do not rely on them to find the best Web sites on your topic, use *subject directories* or meta-sites to enhance value (see below).

Finding Those Diamonds in the Desert: Using Subject Directories and Meta-sites

Although some search engines, like WebCrawler (www.webcrawler.com) do evaluate the Web sites they index, most search engines do not make any judgment on the worth of the content. They just return a long—sometimes very long—list of sites that contained your keyword. However, *subject directories* exist that are developed by human indexers, usually librarians or subject experts, and are defined by Cohen (1999) as follows:

> "A subject directory is a service that offers a collection of links to Internet resources submitted by site creators or evaluators and organized into subject categories. Directory services use selection criteria for choosing links to include, though the selectivity varies among services (p. 27)."

World Wide Web Subject directories are useful when you want to see sites on your topic that have been reviewed, evaluated, and selected for their authority, accuracy, and value. They can be real time savers for students, since subject directories weed out the commercial, lightweight, or biased Web sites.

Metasites are similar to subject directories, but are more specific in nature, usually dealing with one scholarly field or discipline. Some examples of subject directories and meta-sites are found in the table on the next page.

Choose subject directories to ensure that you are searching the highest quality Web pages. As an added bonus, subject directories periodically check Web links to make sure that there are fewer dead ends and out-dated links.

iSearch: Psychology

SMART SEARCHING—SUBJECT DIRECTORIES AND META-SITES

TYPES—SUBJECT DIRECTORIES	EXAMPLES
General, covers many topics	Access to Internet and Subject Resources (www2.lib.udel.edu/subj/) Best Information on the Net (BIOTN) (http://library.sau.edu/bestinfo/) Federal Web Locator (www.infoctr.edu/fwl/) Galaxy (galaxy.einet.net) INFOMINE: Scholarly Internet Resource Collections (infomine.ucr.edu/) InfoSurf: Resources by Subject (www.library.ucsb.edu/subj/) Librarian's Index to the Internet (www.lii.org/) Martindale's "The Reference Desk" (www-sci.lib.uci.edu/HSG/ref.html) PINAKES: A Subject Launchpad (www.hw.ac.uk/libWWW/irn/pinakes/pinakes.html) Refdesk.com (www.refdesk.com) Search Engines and Subject Directories (College of New Jersey) (www.tcnj.edu/~library/research/internet_search.html) Scout Report Archives (www.scout.cs.wisc.edu/archives) Selected Reference Sites (www.mnsfld.edu/depts/lib/mu~ref.html) WWW Virtual Library (http://vlib.org)
Subject Oriented	
• Communication Studies	The Media and Communication Studies Site (www.aber.ac.uk/media) University of Iowa Department of Communication Studies (www.uiowa.edu/~commstud/resources)
• Cultural Studies	Sara Zupko's Cultural Studies Center (www.popcultures.com)
• Education	Educational Virtual Library (www.csu.edu.au/education/library.html) ERIC [Education ResourcesInformation Center] (ericir.sunsite.syr.edu/) Kathy Schrock's Guide for Educators (kathyschrock.net/abceval/index.htm)
• Journalism	Journalism Resources (bailiwick.lib.uiowa.edu/journalism/) Journalism and Media Criticism page (www.chss.montclair.edu/english/furr/media.html)
• Literature	Norton Web Source to American Literature (www.wwnorton.com/naal) Project Gutenberg [Over 3,000 full text titles] (www.gutenberg.net)

SMART SEARCHING, *continued*	
TYPES—SUBJECT DIRECTORIES	EXAMPLES
• Medicine & Health	PubMed [National Library of Medicine's index to Medical journals, 1966 to present] (www.ncbi.nlm.nih.gov/PubMed/) RxList: The Internet Drug Index (rxlist.com) Go Ask Alice (www.goaskalice.columbia.edu) [Health and sexuality]
• Technology	CNET.com (www.cnet.com)

Another closely related group of sites are the *Virtual Library sites,* also referred to as Digital Library sites. Hopefully, your campus library has an outstanding Web site for both on-campus and off-campus access to resources. If not, there are several virtual library sites that you can use, although you should realize that some of the resources would be subscription based, and not accessible unless you are a student of that particular university or college. These are useful because, like the subject directories and meta-sites, experts have organized Web sites by topic and selected only those of highest quality.

You now know how to search for information and use search engines more effectively. In the next section, you will learn more tips for evaluating the information that you found.

VIRTUAL LIBRARY SITES	
PUBLIC LIBRARIES	
• Internet Public Library	www.ipl.org
• Library of Congress	lcweb.loc.gov/homepage/lchp.html
• New York Public Library	www.nypl.org
University/College Libraries	
• Bucknell	jade.bucknell.edu/
• Case Western	www.cwru.edu/uclibraries.html
• Dartmouth	www.dartmouth.edu/~library
• Duke	www.lib.duke.edu/
• Franklin & Marshall	www.library.fandm.edu
• Harvard	www.harvard.edu/museums/
• Penn State	www.libraries.psu.edu
• Princeton	infoshare1.princeton.edu
• Stanford	www.slac.stanford.edu/FIND/spires.html
• ULCA	www.library.ucla.edu

iSearch: Psychology

(continued)

VIRTUAL LIBRARY SITES, *continued*

PUBLIC LIBRARIES

Other
- Perseus Project [subject specific—classics, supported by   www.perseus.tufts.edu
  grants from corporations and educational institutions]

BIBLIOGRAPHY FOR FURTHER READING

Books

Basch, Reva. (1996). Secrets of the Super Net Searchers.

Berkman, Robert I. (2000). *Find It Fast: How to Uncover Expert Information on Any Subject Online or in Print.* NY: HarperResource.

Glossbrenner, Alfred & Glossbrenner, Emily. (1999). *Search Engines for the World Wide Web,* 2nd Ed. Berkeley, CA: Peachpit Press.

Hock, Randolph, & Berinstein, Paula.. (1999). *The Extreme Searcher's Guide to Web Search Engines: A Handbook for the Serious Searcher.* Information Today, Inc.

Miller, Michael. *Complete Idiot's Guide to Yahoo!* (2000). Indianapolis, IN: Que.

Miller, Michael. *Complete Idiot's Guide to Online Search Secrets.* (2000). Indianapolis, IN: Que.

Paul, Nora, Williams, Margot, & Hane, Paula. (1999). *Great Scouts!: CyberGuides for Subject Searching on the Web.* Information Today, Inc.

Radford, Marie, Barnes, Susan, & Barr, Linda (2001). *Web Research: Selecting, Evaluating, and Citing* Boston. Allyn and Bacon.

Journal Articles

Cohen, Laura B. (1999, August). The Web as a research tool: Teaching strategies for instructors. *CHOICE Supplement* 3, 20–44.

Cohen, Laura B. (August 2000). Searching the Web: The Human Element Emerges. *CHOICE Supplement 37,* 17–31.

Introna, Lucas D., & Nissenbaum, Helen. (2000). Shaping the web: Why the politics of search engines matters. The Information Society, Vol. 16, No. 3, pp. 169–185.

Evaluating Sources on the Web

Congratulations! You've found a great Web site. Now what? The Web site you found seems like the perfect Web site for your research. But, are you sure? Why is it perfect? What criteria are you using to determine whether this Web site suits your purpose?

Think about it. Where else on earth can anyone "publish" information regardless of the *accuracy, currency,* or *reliability* of the information? The

Internet has opened up a world of opportunity for posting and distributing information and ideas to virtually everyone, even those who might post misinformation for fun, or those with ulterior motives for promoting their point of view. Armed with the information provided in this guide, you can dig through the vast amount of useless information and misinformation on the World Wide Web to uncover the valuable information. Because practically anyone can post and distribute their ideas on the Web, you need to develop a new set of *critical thinking skills* that focus on the evaluation of the quality of information, rather than be influenced and manipulated by slick graphics and flashy moving java script.

Before the existence of online sources, the validity and accuracy of a source was more easily determined. For example, in order for a book to get to the publishing stage, it must go through many critiques, validation of facts, reviews, editorial changes and the like. Ownership of the information in the book is clear because the author's name is attached to it. The publisher's reputation is on the line too. If the book turns out to have incorrect information, reputations and money can be lost. In addition, books available in a university library are further reviewed by professional librarians and selected for library purchase because of their accuracy and value to students. Journal articles downloaded or printed from online subscription services, such as Infotrac, ProQuest, EbscoHost, or other fulltext databases, are put through the same scrutiny as the paper versions of the journals.

On the World Wide Web, however, Internet service providers (ISPs) simply give Web site authors a place to store information. The Web site author can post information that may not be validated or tested for accuracy. One mistake students typically make is to assume that all information on the Web is of equal value. Also, in the rush to get assignments in on time, students may not take the extra time to make sure that the information they are citing is accurate. It is easy just to cut and paste without really thinking about the content in a critical way. However, to make sure you are gathering accurate information and to get the best grade on your assignments, it is vital that you develop your critical ability to sift through the dirt to find the diamonds.

Web Evaluation Criteria

So, here you are, at this potentially great site. Let's go though some ways you can determine if this site is one you can cite with confidence in your research. Keep in mind, ease of use of a Web site is an issue, but more important is learning how to determine the validity of data, facts, and statements for your use. The five traditional ways to verify a paper source can also be applied to your Web source: *accuracy, authority, objectivity, coverage,* and *currency*.

iSearch: Psychology

Evaluating Web Sites Using
Five Criteria to Judge Web Site Content

Accuracy—How reliable is the information?

Authority—Who is the author and what are his or her credentials?

Objectivity—Does the Web site present a balanced or biased point of view?

Coverage—Is the information comprehensive enough for your needs?

Currency—Is the Web site up to date?

Use additional criteria to judge Web site content, including

- **Publisher, documentation, relevance, scope, audience, appropriateness of format**, and **navigation**
- Judging whether the site is made up of **primary (original) or secondary (interpretive) sources**
- Determining whether the information is **relevant** to your research

Content Evaluation

Accuracy. Internet searches are not the same as searches of library databases because much of the information on the Web has not been edited, whereas information in databases has. It is your responsibility to make sure that the information you use in a school project is accurate. When you examine the content on a Web site or Web page, you can ask yourself a number of questions to determine whether the information is accurate.

1. Is the information reliable?
2. Do the facts from your other research contradict the facts you find on this Web page?
3. Do any misspellings and/or grammar mistakes indicate a hastily put together Web site that has not been checked for accuracy?
4. Is the content on the page verifiable through some other source? Can you find similar facts elsewhere (journals, books, or other online sources) to support the facts you see on this Web page?
5. Do you find links to other Web sites on a similar topic? If so, check those links to ascertain whether they back up the information you see on the Web page you are interested in using.
6. Is a bibliography of additional sources for research provided? Lack of a bibliography doesn't mean the page isn't accurate, but having one allows you further investigation points to check the information.
7. Does the site of a research document or study explain how the data was collected and the type of research method used to interpret the data?

If you've found a site with information that seems too good to be true, it may be. You need to verify information that you read on the Web by cross-checking against other sources.

Authority.   An important question to ask when you are evaluating a Web site is, "Who is the author of the information?" Do you know whether the author is a recognized authority in his or her field? Biographical information, references to publications, degrees, qualifications, and organizational affiliations can help to indicate an author's authority. For example, if you are researching the topic of laser surgery citing a medical doctor would be better than citing a college student who has had laser surgery.

The organization sponsoring the site can also provide clues about whether the information is fact or opinion. Examine how the information was gathered and the research method used to prepare the study or report. Other questions to ask include:

1. Who is responsible for the content of the page? Although a webmaster's name is often listed, this person is not necessarily responsible for the content.
2. Is the author recognized in the subject area? Does this person cite any other publications he or she has authored?
3. Does the author list his or her background or credentials (e.g., Ph.D. degree, title such as professor, or other honorary or social distinction)?
4. Is there a way to contact the author? Does the author provide a phone number or email address?
5. If the page is mounted by an organization, is it a known, reputable one?
6. How long has the organization been in existence?
7. Does the URL for the Web page end in the extension .edu or .org? Such extensions indicate authority compared to dotcoms (.com), which are commercial enterprises. (For example, www.cancer.com takes you to an online drugstore that has a cancer information page; www.cancer.org is the American Cancer Society Web site.)

A good idea is to ask yourself whether the author or organization presenting the information on the Web is an authority on the subject. If the answer is no, this may not be a good source of information.

Objectivity.   Every author has a point of view, and some views are more controversial than others. Journalists try to be objective by providing both sides of a story. Academics attempt to persuade readers by presenting a logical argument, which cites other scholars' work. You need to look for two sided arguments in news and information sites. For academic papers, you need to determine how the paper fits within its discipline and whether the author is using controversial methods for reporting a conclusion.

Authoritative authors situate their work within a larger discipline. This background helps readers evaluate the author's knowledge on a particular

iSearch: Psychology

subject. You should ascertain whether the author's approach is controversial and whether he or she acknowledges this. More important, is the information being presented as fact or opinion? Authors who argue for their position provide readers with other sources that support their arguments. If no sources are cited, the material may be an opinion piece rather than an objective presentation of information. The following questions can help you determine objectivity:

1. Is the purpose of the site clearly stated, either by the author or the organization authoring the site?
2. Does the site give a balanced viewpoint or present only one side?
3. Is the information directed toward a specific group of viewers?
4. Does the site contain advertising?
5. Does the copyright belong to a person or an organization?
6. Do you see anything to indicate who is funding the site?

Everyone has a point of view. This is important to remember when you are using Web resources. A question to keep asking yourself is, What is the bias or point of *view* being expressed here?

Coverage.   Coverage deals with the breadth and depth of information presented on a Web site. Stated another way, it is about how much information is presented and how detailed the information is. Looking at the site map or index can give you an idea about how much information is contained on a site. This isn't necessarily bad. Coverage is a criteria that is tied closely to *your* research requirement. For one assignment, a given Web site may be too general for your needs. For another assignment, that same site might be perfect. Some sites contain very little actual information because pages are filled with links to other sites. Coverage also relates to objectivity You should ask the following questions about coverage:

1. Does the author present both sides of the story or is a piece of the story missing?
2. Is the information comprehensive enough for your needs?
3. Does the site cover too much, too generally?
4. Do you need more specific information than the site can provide?
5. Does the site have an objective approach?

In addition to examining what is covered on a Web site, equally revealing is what is not covered. Missing information can reveal a bias in the material. Keep in mind that you are evaluating the information on a Web site for your research requirements.

Currency.   Currency questions deal with the timeliness of information. However, currency is more important for some topics than for others. For example, currency is essential when you are looking for technology related topics and current events. In contrast, currency may not be relevant when you are doing research on Plato or Ancient Greece. In terms of Web sites, currency also pertains to whether the site is being kept up to date and links are being maintained. Sites on the Web are sometimes abandoned by their owners. When people move or change jobs, they may neglect to remove theft site from the company or university server. To test currency ask the following questions:

1. Does the site indicate when the content was created?
2. Does the site contain a last revised date? How old is the date? (In the early part of 2001, a university updated their Web site with a "last updated" date of 1901! This obviously was a Y2K problem, but it does point out the need to be observant of such things!)
3. Does the author state how often he or she revises the information? Some sites are on a monthly update cycle (e.g., a government statistics page).
4. Can you tell specifically what content was revised?
5. Is the information still useful for your topic? Even if the last update is old, the site might still be worthy of use *if* the content is still valid for your research.

Relevancy to Your Research:
Primary versus Secondary Sources

Some research assignments require the use of primary (original) sources. Materials such as raw data, diaries, letters, manuscripts, and original accounts of events can be considered primary material. In most cases, these historical documents are no longer copyrighted. The Web is a great source for this type of resource.

Information that has been analyzed and previously interpreted is considered a secondary source. Sometimes secondary sources are more appropriate than primary sources. If, for example, you are asked to analyze a topic or to find an analysis of a topic, a secondary source of an analysis would be most appropriate. Ask yourself the following questions to determine whether the Web site is relevant to your research:

1. Is it a primary or secondary source?
2. Do you need a primary source?
3. Does the assignment require you to cite different types of sources? For example, are you supposed to use at least one book, one journal article, and one Web page?

You need to think critically, both visually and verbally, when evaluating Web sites. Because Web sites are designed as multimedia hypertexts, nonlinear texts, visual elements, and navigational tools are added to the evaluation process.

iSearch: Psychology

Help in Evaluating Web Sites.   One shortcut to finding high-quality Web sites is using subject directories and meta-sites, which select the Web sites they index by similar evaluation criteria to those just described. If you want to learn more about evaluating Web sites, many colleges and universities provide sites that help you evaluate Web resources. The following list contains some excellent examples of these evaluation sites:

- Evaluating Quality on the Net—Hope Tillman, Babson College
  www.hopetillman.com/findqual.html
- Critical Web Evaluation—Kurt W. Wagner, William Paterson University of New Jersey
  euphrates.wpunj.edu/faculty/wagnerk/
- Evalation Criteria—Susan Beck, New Mexico State University
  lib.nmsu.edu/instruction/evalcrit.html
- A Student's Guide to Research with the WWW
  www.slu.edu/departments/english/research/
- Evaluating Web Pages: Questions to Ask & Strategies for Getting the Answers
  www.lib.berkeley.edu/TeachingLib/Guides/Internet/EvalQuestions.html

Critical Evaluation Web Sites

WEB SITE AND URL	SOURCE
Critical Thinking in an Online World **www.library.ucsb.edu/untangle/jones.html**	*Paper from "Untangling the Web" 1996*
Educom Review: Information **www.educause.edu/pub/er/review/reviewArticles/31231.html**	*EDUCAUSE Literacy as a Liberal Art (1996 article)*
Evaluating Information Found on the Internet **MiltonsWeb.mse.jhu.edu/research/education/net.html**	*University of Utah Library*
Evaluating Web Sites **www.lib.purdue.edu/InternetEval**	*Purdue University Library*
Evaluating Web Sites **www.lehigh.edu/~inref/guides/evaluating.web.html**	*Lehigh University*
ICONnect: Curriculum Connections Overview **www.ala.org/ICONN/evaluate.html**	*American Library Association's technology education initiative*
Kathy Schrock's ABC's of Web Site Evaluation **www.kathyschrock.net/abceval/**	*Author's Web site*

Kids Pick the best of the Web "Top 10: Announced" **www.ala.org/news/topkidpicks.html**	*American Library Association initiative underwritten by Microsoft (1998)*
Resource Selection and Information Evaluation **alexia.lis.uiuc.edu/~janicke/ InfoAge.html**	*Univ of Illinois, Champaign-Urbana (Librarian)*
Testing the Surf: Criteria for Evaluating Internet Information Sources **info.lib.uh.edu/pr/v8/n3/ smit8n3.html**	*University of Houston Libraries*
Evaluating Web Resources **www2.widener.edu/ Wolfgram-Memorial-Library/ webevaluation/webeval.htm**	*Widener University Library*
UCLA College Library Instruction: Thinking Critically about World Wide Web Resources **www.library.ucla.edu/libraries/ college/help/critical/**	*UCLA Library*
UG OOL: Judging Quality on the Internet **www.open.uoguelph.ca/resources/ skills/judging.html**	*University of Guelph*
Web Evaluation Criteria **lib.nmsu.edu/instruction/ evalcrit.html**	*New Mexico State University Library*
Web Page Credibility Checklist **www.park.pvt.k12.md.us/academics/ research/credcheck.htm**	*Park School of Baltimore*
Evaluating Web Sites for Educational Uses: Bibliography and Checklist **www.unc.edu/cit/guides/irg-49.html**	*University of North Carolina*
Evaluating Web Sites **www.lesley.edu/library/guides/ research/evaluating_web.html**	*Lesley University*

iSearch: Psychology

Tip: Can't seem to get a URL to work? If the URL doesn't begin with www, you may need to put the http:// in front of the URL. Usually, browsers can handle URLs that begin with www without the need to type in the "http://" but if you find you're having trouble, add the http://.

Documentation Guidelines for Online Sources

Your Citation for Exemplary Research

There's another detail left for us to handle—the formal citing of electronic sources in academic papers. The very factor that makes research on the Internet exciting is the same factor that makes referencing these sources challenging: their dynamic nature. A journal article exists, either in print or on microfilm, virtually forever. A document on the Internet can come, go, and change without warning. Because the purpose of citing sources is to allow another scholar to retrace your argument, a good citation allows a reader to obtain information from your primary sources, to the extent possible. This means you need to include not only information on when a source was posted on the Internet (if available) but also when you obtained the information.

The two arbiters of form for academic and scholarly writing are the Modern Language Association (MLA) and the American Psychological Association (APA); both organizations have established styles for citing electronic publications.

MLA Style

In the fifth edition of the *MLA Handbook for Writers of Research Papers,* the MLA recommends the following formats:

- **URLs:** URLs are enclosed in angle brackets (<>) and contain the access mode identifier, the formal name for such indicators as "http" or "ftp." If a URL must be split across two lines, break it only after a slash (/). Never introduce a hyphen at the end of the first line. The URL should include all the parts necessary to identify uniquely the file/document being cited.

    `<http://www.csun.edu/~rtvfdept/home/index.html>`

- **An online scholarly project or reference database:** A complete "online reference contains the title of the project or database (underlined); the name of the editor of the project or database (if given); electronic publication information, including version number (if relevant and if not part of the title), date of electronic publication or latest update, and name of any sponsoring institution or organization; date of access; and electronic address.

    <u>The Perseus Project</u>. Ed. Gregory R. Crane. Mar. 1997. Department of Classics, Tufts University. 15 June 1998 <http://www.perseus.tufts.edu/>.

If you cannot find some of the information, then include the information that is available. The MLA also recommends that you print or download electronic documents, freezing them in time for future reference.

- **A document within a scholarly project or reference database:** It is much more common to use only a portion of a scholarly project or database. To cite an essay, poem, or other short work, begin this citation with the name of the author and the title of the work (in quotation marks). Then, include all the information used when citing a complete online scholarly project or reference database, however, make sure you use the URL of the specific work and not the address of the general site.

Cuthberg, Lori. "Moonwalk: Earthlings' Finest Hour." <u>Discovery Channel Online</u>. 1999. Discovery Channel. 25 Nov. 1999 <http://www.discovery.com/ indep/newsfeatures/moonwalk/challenge.html>.

- **A professional or personal site:** Include the name of the person creating the site (reversed), followed by a period, the title of the site (underlined), or, if there is no title, a description such as Home page (such a description is neither placed in quotes nor underlined). Then, specify the name of any school, organization, or other institution affiliated with the site and follow it with your date of access and the URL of the page.

Packer, Andy. Home page. 1Apr. 1998 <http:// www.suu.edu/~students/Packer.htm>.

Some electronic references are truly unique to the online domain. These include email, newsgroup postings, MUDs (multiuser domains) or MOOs (multiuser domains, object-oriented), and IRCs (Internet Relay Chats).

Email. In citing email messages, begin with the writer's name (reversed) followed by a period, then the title of the message (if any) in quotations as it appears in the subject line. Next comes a description of the message, typically "Email to," and the recipient (e.g., "the author"), and finally the date of the message.

Davis, Jeffrey. "Web Writing Resources." Email to Nora Davis. 3 Jan. 2000.

Sommers, Laurice. "Re: College Admissions Practices." Email to the author. 12 Aug. 1998.

List Servers and Newsgroups.   In citing these references, begin with the author's name (reversed) followed by a period. Next include the title of the document (in quotes) from the subject line, followed by the words "Online posting" (not in quotes). Follow this with the date of posting. For list servers, include the date of access, the name of the list (if known), and the online address of the list's moderator or administrator. For newsgroups, follow "Online posting" with the date of posting, the date of access, and the name of the newsgroup, prefixed with "news:" and enclosed in angle brackets.

Applebaum, Dale. "Educational Variables." Online
    posting. 29 Jan. 1998. Higher Education
    Discussion Group. 30 Jan. 1993
    <jlucidoj@unc.edu>.

Gostl, Jack. "Re: Mr. Levitan." Online posting.
    13 June 1997. 20 June 1997
    <news:alt.edu.bronxscience>.

MUDs, MOOs, and IRCs.   Begin with the name of the speaker(s) followed by a period. Follow with the description and date of the event, the forum in which the communication took place, the date of access, and the online address. If you accessed the MOO or MUD through telnet, your citation might appear as follows:

Guest. Personal interview. 13 Aug. 1998.
    <telnet://du.edu:8888>.

For more information on MLA documentation style for online sources, check out their Web site at http://www.mla.org/style/sources.htm.

APA Style

The newly revised *Publication Manual of the American Psychological Association* (5th ed.) now includes guidelines for Internet resources. The manual recommends that, at a minimum, a reference of an Internet source should provide a document title or description, a date (either the date of publication or update or the date of retrieval), and an address (in Internet terms, a uniform resource locator, or URL). Whenever possible, identify the authors of a document as well. It's important to remember that, unlike the MLA, the APA does not include temporary or transient sources (e.g., letters, phone calls, etc.) in its "References" page, preferring to handle them in the text. The general suggested format is as follows:

Online periodical:

```
Author, A. A., Author, B. B., & Author, C. C.
   (2000). Title of article. Title of Periodical,
   xx, xxxxx. Retrieved month, day, year, from
   source.
```

Online document:

```
Author, A. A. (2000). Title of work. Retrieved
   month, day, year, from source.
```

Some more specific examples are as follows:

FTP (File Transfer Protocol) Sites. To cite files available for down-loading via FTP, give the author's name (if known), the publication date (if available and if different from the date accessed), the full title of the paper (capitalizing only the first word and proper nouns), the date of access, and the address of the FTP site along with the full path necessary to access the file.

```
Deutsch, P. (1991) Archie: An electronic directory
   service for the Internet. Retrieved January 25,
   2000 from File Transfer Protocol: ftp://
   ftp.sura.net/pub/archie/docs/whatis.archie
```

WWW Sites (World Wide Web). To cite files available for viewing or downloading via the World Wide Web, give the author's name (if known), the year of publication (if known and if different from the date accessed), the full title of the article, and the title of the complete work (if applicable) in italics. Include any additional information (such as versions, editions, or revisions) in parentheses immediately following the title. Include the date of retrieval and full URL (the http address).

```
Burka, L. P. (1993). A hypertext history of multi-
   user dungeons. MUDdex. Retrieved January 13, 1997
   from the World Wide Web: http://www.utopia.com/
   talent/lpb/muddex/essay/
```

```
Tilton, J. (1995). Composing good HTML (Vers. 2.0.6).
   Retrieved December 1, 1996 from the World Wide Web:
   http://www.cs.cmu.edu/~tilt/cgh/
```

Synchronous Communications (MOOs, MUDs, IRC, etc.). Give the name of the speaker(s), the complete date of the conversation being referenced in parentheses, and the title of the session (if applicable). Next,

iSearch: Psychology

list the title of the site in italics, the protocol and address (if applicable), and any directions necessary to access the work. Last, list the date of access, followed by the retrieval information. Personal interviews do not need to be listed in the References, but do need to be included in parenthetic references in the text (see the APA *Publication Manual*).

```
Cross, J. (1996, February 27). Netoric's Tuesday
    "cafe: Why use MUDs in the writing classroom?
    MediaMoo. Retrieved March 1, 1996 from File
    Transfer Protocol: ftp://daedalus.com/
    pub/ACW/NETORIC/catalog
```

Gopher Sites.   List the author's name (if applicable), the year of publication, the title of the file or paper, and the title of the complete work (if applicable). Include any print publication information (if available) followed by the protocol (i.e., gopher://). List the date that the file was accessed and the path necessary to access the file.

```
Massachusetts Higher Education Coordinating Council.
    (1994). Using coordination and collaboration to
    address change. Retrieved July 16, 1999 from the
    World Wide Web: gopher://gopher.mass.edu:170/
    00gopher_root%3A%5B_hecc%5D_plan
```

Email, Listservs, and Newsgroups.   Do not include personal email in the list of References. Although unretrievable communication such as email is not included in APA References, somewhat more public or accessible Internet postings from newsgroups or listservs may be included. See the APA *Publication Manual* for information on in-text citations.

```
Heilke, J. (1996, May 3). Webfolios. Alliance for
    Computers and Writing Discussion List. Retrieved
    December 31, 1996 from the World Wide Web:
    http://www.ttu.edu/lists/acw-1/9605/0040.html
```

Other authors and educators have proposed similar extensions to the APA style. You can find links to these pages at:

```
www.psychwww.com/resource/apacrib.htm
```

Remember, "frequently-referenced" does not equate to "correct" "or even "desirable." Check with your professor to see if your course or school has a preference for an extended APA style.

Web Activities

Internet Activities for Psychology

At the most basic level, psychologists are interested in understanding behavior and mental processes. Although this sounds relatively simple, just think about the seemingly infinite number of factors that influence your behavior and thought processes throughout a single day. It is these near infinite number of factors that make psychology such a diverse discipline. For example, some psychologists study behavior at the neurochemical or genetic level, while others study behavior as it occurs in large social networks. Of course, there are also psychologists that study everything in between. Although this degree of diversity adds some additional challenges to the study of psychology, it also makes it that much more intriguing. In the study of psychology, there is something for everyone.

The scientific study of psychology can be broadly characterized as either applied or basic. While most students are interested in applying psychological principles, like reducing stress, treating mental disorders, or understanding family dynamics, it is the research component of psychology that provides the foundation for all aspects of psychology. The basic science side addresses questions like why do people become dependent upon drugs, how do social networks influence decision making, or what are the biological underpinnings of aggression. Additionally, without basic science research, there would be no means by which to assess what is being applied. That is, how do you know that one particular method of therapy actually works? Without basic science, psychology would amount to no more than educated guesses and superstition.

The History of Psychology

When you meet new people, what type of questions generally come to mind? Usually, it is nice to know a little about where they grew up. Perhaps it would be beneficial to know what school they attended. Also, you would likely ask what they do for a living. As a person new to the field of psychology, wouldn't it also be interesting to learn something about the people who helped make psychology what it is today. Thus, to get a good overview of the discipline of psychology, describe interesting facts about each of the following psychologists: (**http://www.pbs.org/wgbh/aso/databank/humbeh.html**)

• Jean-Martin Charcot

_____

_____

_____

A Science Odyssey: People and Discoveries: Human Behavior - Microsoft Internet Explorer

File Edit View Favorites Tools Help

Back • → • ⊗ ⊗ ⌂ ⊗ Search Favorites Media ⊗ ⊗ ⊗ ⊗ ⊗ ⊗

Address http://www.pbs.org/wgbh/aso/databank/humbeh.html

PEOPLE AND DISCOVERIES

Human Behavior

People
Jean-Martin Charcot
Charles Davenport
Sigmund Freud
Frieda Fromm-Reichmann
Harry Harlow
Abraham Maslow
Ivan Pavlov
Wilder Penfield
B.F. Skinner
Roger Sperry
John Watson

Discoveries
1900	Freud's book, "The Interpretation of Dreams" released
1905	Binet pioneers intelligence testing
1913	Watson launches behaviorist school of psychology
1923	Eugenics movement reaches its height
1923 - 1952	Piaget describes stages of cognitive development
1935	Moniz develops lobotomy for mental illness
1938	Electroshock therapy introduced

iSearch: Psychology

- Charles Davenport

  _____

  _____

  _____

- Sigmund Freud

  _____

  _____

  _____

- Frieda Fromm-Reichmann

  _____

  _____

  _____

- Harry Harlow

  _____

  _____

  _____

- Abraham Maslow

  _____

  _____

  _____

- Ivan Pavlov

  _____

  _____

  _____

- Wilder Penfield

  _____

  _____

  _____

- B. F. Skinner

  _____

  _____

  _____

iSearch: Psychology

- Roger Sperry

  _____

  _____

  _____

- John Watson

  _____

  _____

  _____

Of the discoveries listed on the same page, which one do you believe was the most revolutionary to psychology and why?

_____

_____

_____

_____

_____

Careers in Psychology

The Occupational Outlook Handbook from the U.S. Department of Labor, Bureau of Labor Statistics, provides information about the various positions that many psychologists occupy. What are the defining features for each one of these specialty areas within psychology? (**http://stats.bls.gov/ oco/ocos056.htm**)

- Clinical psychologists

  _____

  _____

  _____

- Counseling psychologists

  _____

  _____

  _____

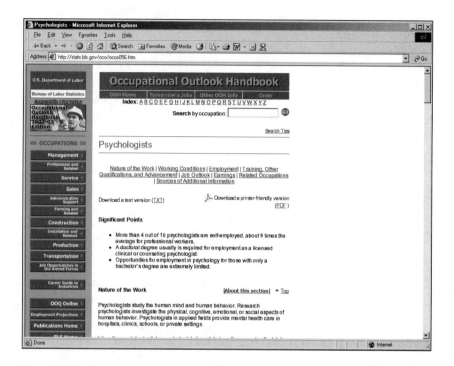

- School psychologists

_____

_____

_____

- Industrial-organizational (I/O) psychologists

_____

_____

_____

- Developmental psychologists

_____

_____

_____

- Social psychologists

  _____

  _____

  _____

- Experimental or research psychologists

  _____

  _____

  _____

What type of education/degree is required for these positions, and how much time does it typically take to earn such a degree?

_____

_____

_____

How much money do psychologists make?

_____

_____

_____

Many psychologists seek employment outside of conventional areas. Of the following non-academic positions, which one do you find the most appealing and why? (**http://www.apa.org/science/nonacad_careers. html**)

Research in Psychology

Many psychologists gain an understanding about behavior by conducting research. Many research projects can take the form of questionnaires or surveys. Sometimes the best way to learn about research is to be a subject in an actual experiment. The following link provides a list of online experiments that are grouped by subject. Select an experiment that seems interesting to you and evaluate how it feels to be the "guinea pig." (**http://psych.hanover.edu/APS/exponnet.html**)

Which research area did you select and why?

_____

_____

_____

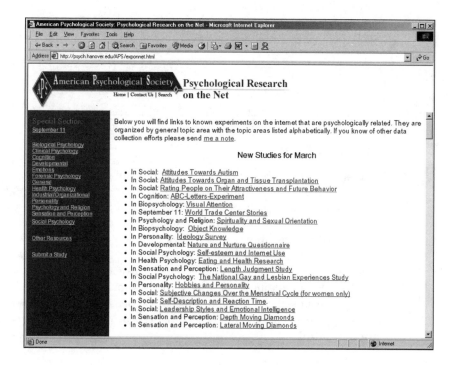

What experiment did you participate in and why?

_____

_____

_____

Was being a research subject a positive, negative, or neutral experience?

_____

_____

_____

Could you easily determine the primary objective of the experiment? If yes, what was it?

_____

_____

_____

iSearch: Psychology

Do you believe that by participating in an experiment you may have helped increase the knowledge base in that particular area of psychology?

_____

_____

_____

Research Ethics

A quote from the APA concerning research with nonhuman subjects; "Psychology encompasses a broad range of areas of research and applied endeavors. Important parts of these endeavors are teaching and research on the behavior of nonhuman animals, which contribute to the understanding of basic principles underlying behavior and to advancing the welfare of both human and nonhuman animals. Clearly, psychologists should conduct their teaching and research in a manner consonant with relevant laws and regulations. In addition, ethical concerns mandate that psychologists should consider the costs and benefits of procedures involving animals before proceeding with the research." (**http://www.apa.org/science/anguide.html**)

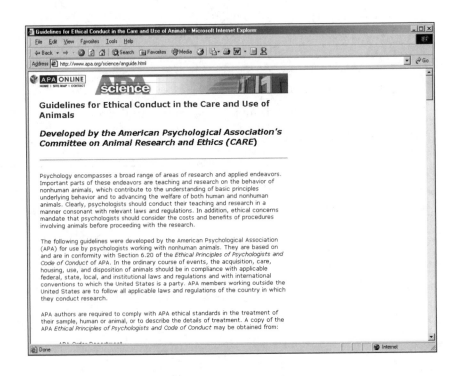

What five justifications are necessary for using animals as research subjects?

_____

_____

_____

_____

Which animals are inappropriate to use as subjects?

_____

_____

What are the guidelines in terms of releasing research subjects into the wild after their use?

_____

_____

Is it worth it? That is, should humans use animals in research?

_____

_____

Do humans research participants receive the same level of protection as animals? One might suspect that humans would receive greater protection, but this is generally not the case. (**http://www.medicalpost.com/mdlink/english/members/medpost/data/3508/01B.htm**)

Are there more mechanisms in place that protect animals then there are to protect humans?

_____

_____

Should the guidelines for human research subjects be tightened or should the requirements for animal subjects be lessened, or should there be no change?

_____

_____

iSearch: Psychology

Would you ever volunteer to be a research subject in an experiment?

_____

_____

_____

Biological Basis of Behavior

Few things in the universe are as mysterious as the human brain. Even to-day with our extensive imaging technology, the brain's complexity still continues to marvel and elude psychologists. Biological psychologists have been studying the brain for decades now and have gained an appreciation for many brain-behavior relationships; that is, which parts of the brain controls which aspects of behavior. Go to the following site and examine some of these brain-behavior relationships. (**http://www.csuchico.edu/psy/ BioPsych/brain.html**) In figure one, what are the names of the first and seventh structure and what are they said to do?

In figure two, what are the names of the second and sixth structure and what are they said to do?

_____

_____

_____

In figure three, what is the name of the second structure and what is it said to do?

_____

_____

_____

In figure four, what is the name of the fourth structure and what is it said to do?

_____

_____

_____

Explore some of the other structures and label their structure and function.

_____

_____

_____

iSearch: Psychology

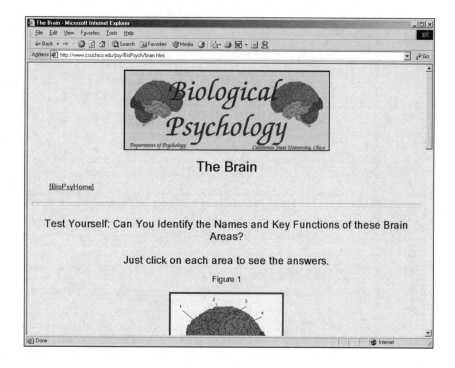

I am sure you have heard the phrase, "you never know what you have until it is gone." This is definitely true when it comes to our mental abilities. We assume that our brain will continue to work as it always has, but this may not necessarily be the case. Unfortunately, many people in our country have suffered and continue to suffer from some sort of injury to their brain. There are a number of non-profit groups that study brain injury. One such group is the Brain Injury Association, whose mission is to create a better future through brain injury prevention, research, education and advocacy. Spend a couple of minutes answering the questions below about brain injury. (**http://www.biausa.org/costsand.htm**)

What are TBI and ABI?

_____

_____

_____

_____

_____

How many Americans are affected by brain injury each year?

_____

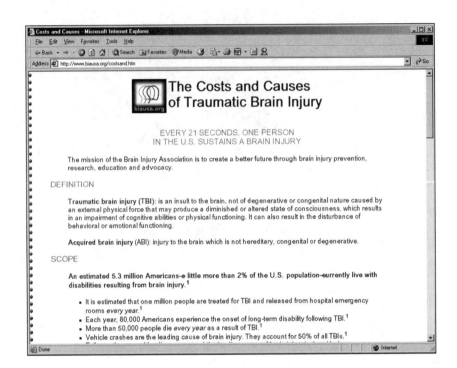

What is the leading cause of brain injury in America?

_____

_____

_____

What age group is at greatest risk for TBI?

_____

_____

_____

How much do brain injuries cost each year in the United States?

_____

_____

Write down two cognitive, physical, and emotional consequences to brain injury.

_____

_____

_____

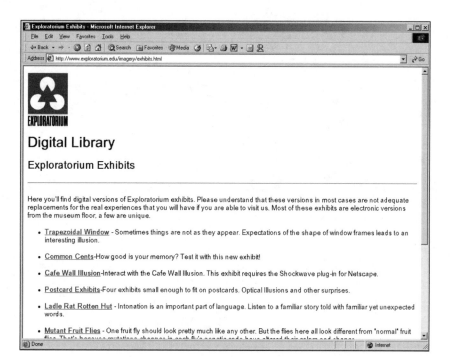

Sensation and Perception

Exploratorium

Go to **http://www.exploratorium.edu/imagery/exhibits.html** and explore three different kinds of illusions. Most of these exhibits are electronic versions from the museum floor; a few are unique.

Which of the many types of illusions do you find the most interesting?

_____

_____

_____

Which specific illusion was the most interesting and why?

_____

_____

_____

After exploring this page do you think seeing is believing?

_____

_____

_____

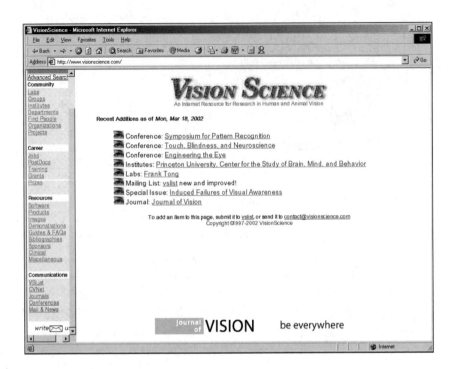

Next, go to the visual illusions page (**http://www.visionscience. com/VisionScience.html**).

What was your favorite illusion?

_____

_____

_____

How is the illusion thought to work?

_____

_____

_____

States of Consciousness

Although behavioral scientists cannot fully explain sleep, they do know that it is essential to our survival. Sleep is a very important state of consciousness. As college students, many of you are not getting the amount of sleep your body and brain needs. Go to the National Sleep Foundation

iSearch: Psychology

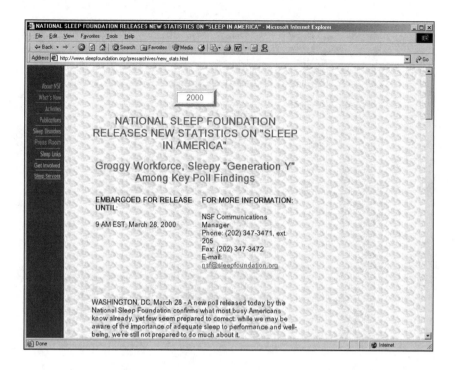

and learn about one of our most important states of consciousness. (**http://www.sleepfoundation.org/pressarchives/new_stats.html**)

How much sleep do most people need?

_____

_____

_____

What is the percentage of young adults that suffer from significant daytime sleepiness?

_____

_____

_____

How many American adults experience a sleep problem a few nights per week or more?

_____

_____

_____

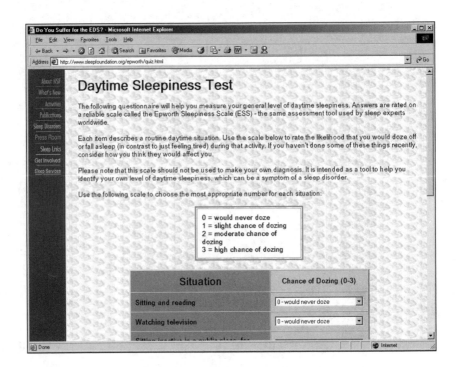

Use the following links to test your knowledge of sleep and determine whether or not you are sleep deprived. (**http://www.sleepfoundation. org/epworth/quiz.html**)

How well did you do?

_____

_____

_____

Are you sleep deprived? If yes, why?

_____

_____

_____

Which adverse effects of sleep deprivation most readily influence you?

_____

_____

_____

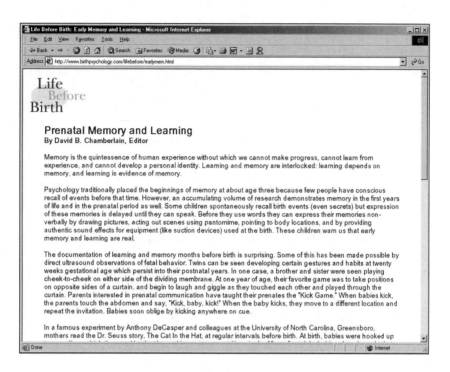

Memory and Learning

While many developmental psychologists would point to the first several years of a persons life to be some of the most important, scientists are know beginning to understand that many important aspects of learning begin even earlier. A series of recent experiments have begun to unravel the mysteries surrounding the origin of human memory, it and appears the much learning takes place during prenatal development. (**http://www. birthpsychology.com/lifebefore/earlymem.html**)

How does one measure prenatal learning?

_____

_____

_____

When is a fetus capable of hearing?

_____

_____

_____

What fact about prenatal learning do you find the most interesting or surprising and why?

_____

_____

_____

How good is your memory? Go to the following link and try to duplicate some simple drawings. Keep track of how well you do. If you don't have Shockwave™, then you will have to install it—don't worry it's free. (**http://www.exploratorium.edu/exhibits/droodles/index.html**)

Number correct on trial one: _____

Number correct on trial two: _____

How well do you remember the image on a penny? Can you identify the correct penny—most people cannot. (**http://www.exploratorium. edu/exhibits/common_cents/index.html**)

Which one did you pick? _____

Which one was the correct choice? _____

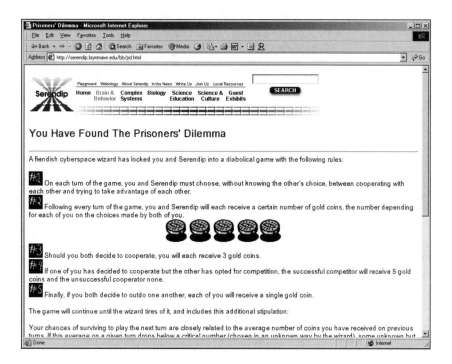

Cognition and Intelligence

This is a variation of what is typically referred to as the "prisoners dilemma game." The scenario is very simple, do you cooperate or compete. Try the game, and keep track of your performance. (**http://serendip. brynmawr.edu/bb/pd.html**)

What are the benefits of cooperating? What are the benefits of competing?

_____

_____

_____

_____

_____

Try one game by just cooperating. How well did you do?

_____

_____

_____

Try one game by only competing. How well did you do?

_____

_____

_____

Now, try to develop the best possible strategy. Did you do better or worse compared to the two scenarios above?

_____

_____

_____

How smart are you? Do Intelligence Quotients (IQ) really measure your intelligence? Take this simple, true-and-false test and see how you do. (**http://www.onlinepsych.com/public/Mind_Games/iq03.htm**)

What was your score? _____

Do you believe that this 20-item test really measures IQ? Why or why not?

_____

_____

_____

How Smart Are You? - Microsoft Internet Explorer

File Edit View Favorites Tools Help

⇐ Back ▾ ⇒ ▾ ⊗ ⌂ ⌂ | ⊚ Search 📷 Favorites ⊕ Media ⌛ | ⬛▾ ⬛ ⬛ ▾ ⬛ ⎘

Address ⬛ http://www.onlinepsych.com/public/Mind_Games/iq03.htm ▾ ⇒ Go

You may select one answer per question

1. Man has no choice but to seek truth. he is made comfortable and frustrated without truth-- thus the quest for truth is part of what makes us _____ ?
   1. ○ noble
   2. ○ different
   3. ○ human
   4. ○ intelligent
   5. ○ aggressive

2. If m is an even integer, then the following is the sum of the next two even integers ?
   1. ○ 2m + 4
   2. ○ 2m + 6
   3. ○ 2m + 8
   4. ○ 2m + 10
   5. ○ 2m + 12

3. Car X traveled from A to B in 30 minutes. The first half of the trip was covered at 50 mph, and the second half at 60 mph. What was the average speed ?
   1. ○ 200/11
   2. ○ 400/11
   3. ○ 500/11

☒ Click

Next Quiz ➡

⬛ Done   🔵 Internet

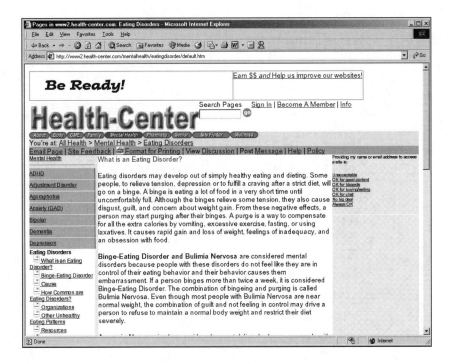

Motivation and Emotion

Many of us have either observed the behavior of others or our own behavior and wondered, "Do I have an eating disorder?" Go to **http://site. health-center.com/brain/eatingdisorder/default.htm** and go to several links that might answer this question.

What is anorexia nervosa and how is it defined?

_____

_____

_____

What is bulimia and how is it defined?

_____

_____

_____

What course of action should you take if you know someone with these behaviors, whether a friend or yourself?

_____

_____

_____

The National Institute on Alcohol Abuse and Alcoholism has put together several fact sheets about the effects of alcohol on one's overall health. The first fact-sheet is on the relationship between stress and alcohol use, while the second one is on college drinking. (**http://www.niaaa.nih.gov/publications/aa32.htm**)

What is meant by a "stress response?"

_____

_____

_____

Does alcohol actually reduce stress?

_____

_____

_____

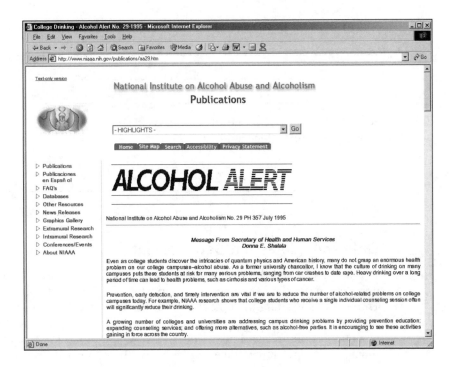

What are some of the long-term consequences of using alcohol as a "medication" to reduce stress?

_____

_____

_____

Go to **http://www.niaaa.nih.gov/publications/aa29.htm**. What is "binge drinking?"

_____

_____

_____

What are some of the negative consequences of drinking to excess while in college?

_____

_____

_____

What factors motivate college students, in particular, to drink?

_____

_____

_____

What is thought to be one of the most effective ways to curb excessive drinking among college students?

_____

_____

_____

Child and Adolescent Development

"We invite you to take a most incredible interactive journey through the first nine months of a baby's development—from conception to birth. Through this exciting multimedia presentation, you will explore and experience baby Emma's development, as seen through the eyes of her parents, Joseph and Deanna." This is a very well done informative presentation. (**http://www.parentsplace.com/first9months/main.html**)

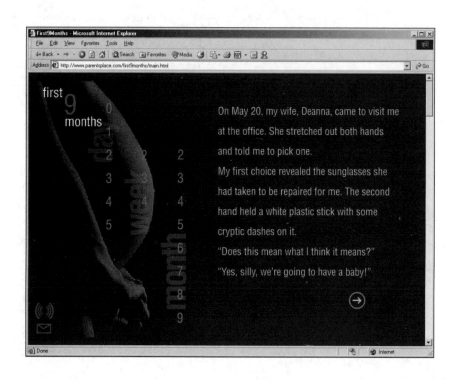

Write done something new that you learned about the first trimester.

_____

_____

_____

Write down something new that you learned about the second trimester.

_____

_____

_____

Write down something new that you learned about the third trimester.

_____

_____

_____

Overall, what was the most interesting piece of information or image that you found on this site?

_____

_____

_____

While it is certainly hard to believe, child abuse has increased dramatically in recent decades in the United States. This trend is especially disturbing when you take into account the enormous energy and money our country has invested in educating, preventing, and treating this terrible problem. Studying the relationship between child-abuse and family structure has provided a lot of insight into this problem. You can explore this problem at the following site. (**http://www.heritage.org/library/categories/family/bg1115.html**)

Since 1980, abuse and neglect of American children has increased by what amount?

_____

_____

According to this report, how much has physical abuse increased since 1980? Similarly, how much has childhood sexual abuse increased since 1980?

_____

_____

_____

iSearch: Psychology

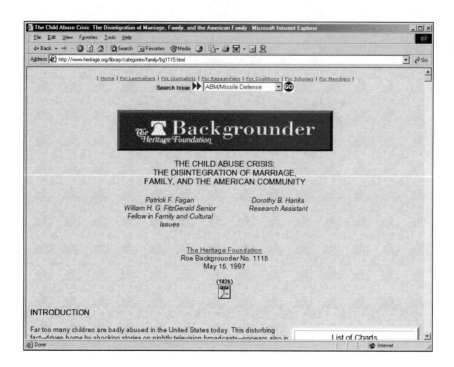

What is the relationship between income and child-abuse?

_____

_____

_____

What is the relationship between marital status and child-abuse? What is typically the best and worst environment for children?

_____

_____

_____

What does the article suggest as a possible solution to this growing problem? What is your opinion?

_____

_____

_____

iSearch: Psychology

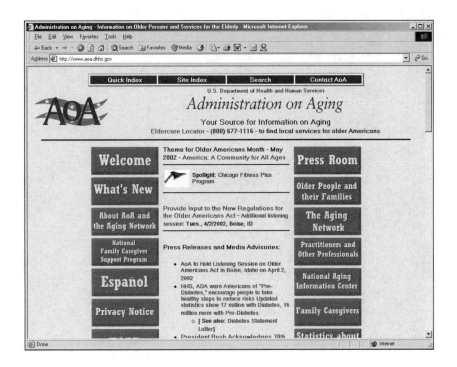

Adult Development and Aging

Go to **http://www.aoa.dhhs.gov/**. What are the three major problems or concerns you could expect to face as a parent or grandparent ages? The information on this URL will guide you to specific concerns for individuals who are aging.

1. _____

2. _____

3. _____

By the time you reach retirement, which of these three problem areas mentioned above will no longer be a concern because of discoveries in the sciences or psychology? Which of these areas will not be a problem to you and why?

_____

_____

_____

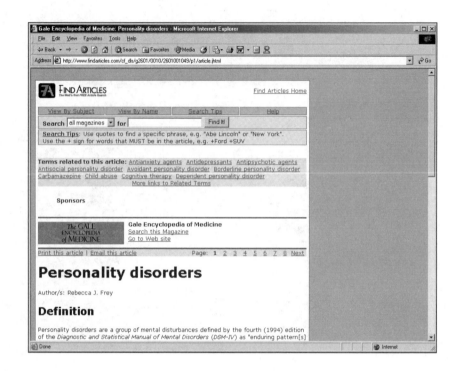

Personality

There are ten different personality disorders. While some of these may be familiar to you (e.g., borderline), there are probably some that you have never even heard of (e.g., schizotypal). Check this link for information about the symptoms that constitute each of these disorders. Select three of the disorders. Define and describe the symptoms for disorder you selected. (**http://www.findarticles.com/cf_dls/g2601/0010/2601001049/p1/ article.jhtml**)

1. _____

2. _____

3. _____

_____

_____

_____

_____

_____

iSearch: Psychology

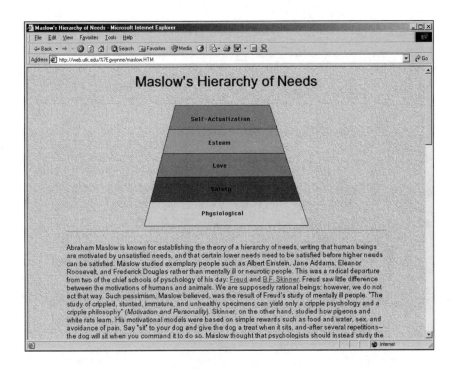

Abraham Maslow developed a now famous model describing human motivation. People are thought to move through various stages, as certain needs are meet. (**http://web.utk.edu/%7Egwynne/maslow.htm**)

What is the hierarchy of needs according to Maslow?

_____

_____

_____

How was his model different from that of his predecessors Freud and Skinner?

_____

_____

_____

What moves people from one level to another?

_____

_____

_____

Do you agree with this model? Why or why not?

_____

_____

_____

Comparing Freud and Jung

Two of the major figures in psychology in the first half of this century are Sigmund Freud and Carl Jung. Both were concerned with personality theories and abnormal behavior. Go to **http://www.cgjungpage.org/** for Jung and **http://www.nypsa.org/** for Freud. Use these sites as starting points to explore the philosophy and theories of both psychologists.

How did Freud and Jung differ in their approach to personality?

_____

_____

_____

_____

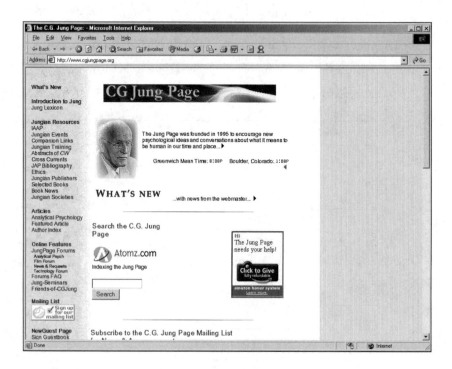

How did Freud and Jung agree in their approach to personality?

_____

_____

_____

_____

What aspect of each psychologist's theories did you find most interesting?

_____

_____

Stress and Health

How healthy is your lifestyle? Most people believe that they are living fairly health lives; however, many people are in fact putting themselves at risk. (**http://www.psychtests.com/tests/minitests/lifestyle_access.html**)

What was your score out of a 100? _____

What advice did you receive?

_____

_____

_____

Do you believe that this 25-item test accurately measured the degree of "health" in your current lifestyle?

_____

_____

_____

Does being part of a religious group actually increase your life expectancy? Does having an active faith decrease your risk for premature death? There is a growing body of research indicating a positive relationship between faith and health. See **http://www.davidmyers.org/ religion/stresshealth.html**

What did one study of 91,909 persons in one county in Maryland find in terms of religious service attendance and death?

_____

_____

_____

What are some of the explanations for longer life expectancies among religious persons?

_____

_____

_____

Overall, do you feel the evidence indicating that religious involvement increases health and longevity are strong?

_____

_____

_____

The Longevity Game

How long will you live? This question has been considered since individuals started thinking. You have information about your parents' and grandparents' longevity. Is their longevity a good indicator of your

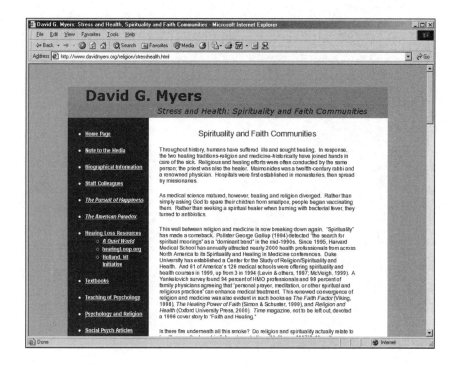

longevity or are other factors as important? The Longevity Game allows you to assess your own probabilities of reaching a specific age based on your life style. Go to **http://www.northwesternmutual.com/games/longevity/** and proceed with the questions.

How long are you projected to live? _____

Are you shocked, happy or surprised by the calculated number? Explain

_____

_____

_____

_____

What factors are the most positive? What factors are the most negative?

_____

_____

_____

_____

What life style factors could you change to increase your estimated longevity?

_____

_____

Return to the game and change some of the life style factors for which you received the largest negative numbers on the summary table. How much did these life style changes affect your estimated life span?

_____

_____

Are these life style changes worth the effort involved in making them in order to add years to your longevity?

_____

_____

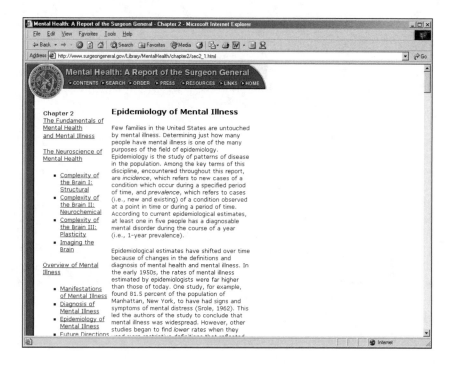

Psychological Disorders and Treatment

Psychopathology (often inappropriately referred to as insanity or being crazy) describes abnormal behavior in scientific terms. Psychopathology involves patterns of thought, emotion, and behavior that are maladaptive, disruptive, or uncomfortable either for the person affected or for others. Just like many people in our country suffer from problems of the heart, back, or muscles, many people also suffer from problems of the brain. What many people don't know is that many of these problems can be treated. (**http://www.surgeongeneral.gov/Library/MentalHealth/chapter2/sec2_1.html**)

What is the difference between "incidence" and "prevalence?"

_____

_____

_____

_____

_____

_____

How many adults in the U.S. suffer from a mental disorder in any given one-year period?

_____

About how many children in the U.S. have a mental disorder?

_____

What is the most common mental disorder among adults and children?

_____

Do older adults suffer from mental disorders at the same rate as younger Americans?

_____

_____

_____

What is the cost of mental illness on our society?

_____

_____

_____

Go to the following site for an overview of anxiety disorders. The major symptoms for each disorder are available for each condition, as is the available treatment. (**http://www.nimh.nih.gov/soundlikeyou.htm**)

Which appears to be the worst condition?

_____

_____

_____

Do you feel you or someone you know may have one of these conditions?

_____

_____

_____

"This test is designed to evaluate your general level of anxiety. Examine the following statements and indicate how often you feel that way." Your level of anxiety will be evaluated and a score will be provided along a 0 to 100, with 100 being very anxious. (**http://www.psychtests.com/ tests/health/anxiety_r_access.html**) The following test is designed to assess your level of depression. (**http://www.depression-screening.**

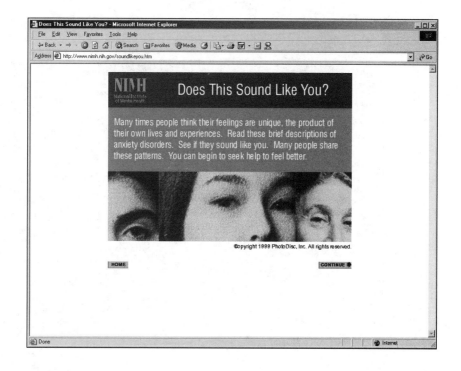

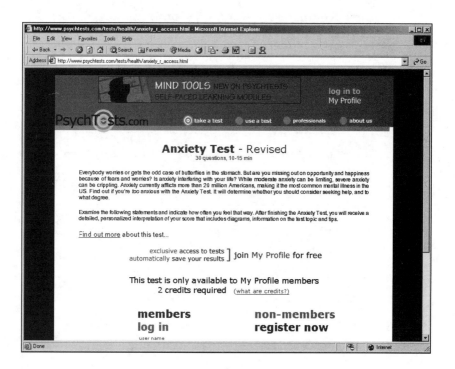

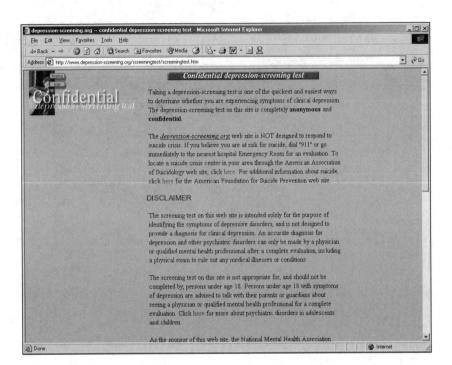

iSearch: Psychology

org/screeningtest/screeningtest.htm) Pick one of these tests and see how you score.

What was your score and what does it mean?

_____

_____

_____

Do you believe that you have a problem with anxiety or depression?

_____

_____

_____

Do you believe that the test you took was valid?

_____

_____

_____

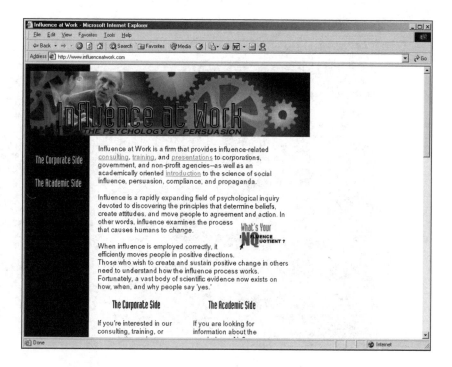

Social Psychology

Social Influence

Go to **http://www.influenceatwork.com/**. This web site is devoted to social influence—the modern, scientific study of persuasion, compliance, and propaganda.

What information at this site did you find most interesting?

_____

_____

_____

What techniques did you learn from this site to help yourself guard against social influence pressures?

_____

_____

_____

As a student you are probably bombarded, from a multiple sources, with facts, figures, anecdotes, and opinions about a variety of ideas. How

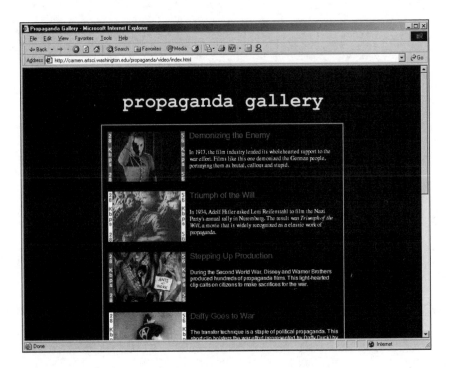

can you separate science from fiction or a rationale argument from propaganda? "This web-site discusses various propaganda techniques, provides contemporary examples of their use, and proposes strategies of mental self-defense." Go to the following link and watch two of the eight commercials and see if you can detect the subtle or not so subtle message. (**http://carmen.artsci.washington.edu/propaganda/video/index. html**)

What video clip did you watch first, and why did you select that particular video?

_____

_____

_____

What was the message? Was it really propaganda?

_____

_____

_____

What video clip did you watch second, and why did you select that particular video?

_____

_____

_____

What was the message? Was it really propaganda?

_____

_____

_____

Applied Psychology

"Sport psychology is (a) the study of the psychological and mental factors that influence and are influenced by participation and performance in sport, exercise, and physical activity, and (b) the application of the knowledge gained through this study to everyday settings. Sport psychology professionals are interested in how participation in sport, exercise, and physical activity may enhance personal development and well-being throughout the life span. Sport psychologists are also involved in assisting coaches in working with athletes as well as helping improve athletes' motivation." Sport psychology is a new and growing field, so take a couple of minutes and examine this site to see if this area of psychology interests you. (**http://www.wcupa.edu/_ACADEMICS/sch_cas.psy/Career_Paths/Sports/Career07.htm**)

What was the first scholarly journal devoted to sport psychology, when was it established, and what is its title?

_____

_____

_____

How is "imagery" used in sport psychology?

_____

_____

_____

What types of jobs can a sports psychologist hold?

_____

_____

_____

iSearch: Psychology

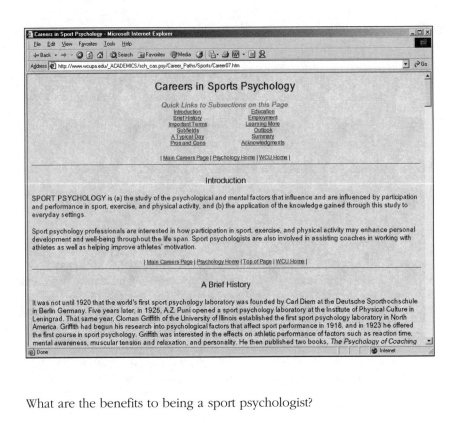

What are the benefits to being a sport psychologist?

_____

_____

_____

What are the drawbacks to being a sport psychologist?

_____

_____

_____

Human Factors psychology is a discipline that addresses the interface between human and machine. Human factors psychologists ask the question, how could the design of something be improved or easier to understand. This site provides "a scrapbook of illustrated examples of things that are hard to use because they do not follow human factors principles." (**http://www.baddesigns.com/examples.html**) Pick three bad designs and explain their problem and the suggested solution.

1. _____

2. _____

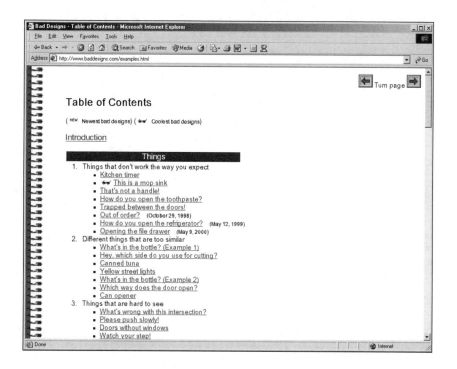

3. _____

_____

_____

_____

_____

_____

_____

iSearch: Psychology

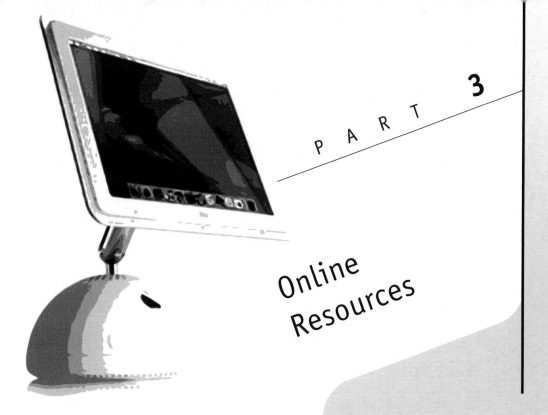

Online Resources

Internet Sites Useful in Psychology

Introduction, Research, and History of Psychology

CyberPsychlink

`http://cctr.umkc.edu/user/dmartin/psych2.html`

CyberPsychLink is an Extensive Resource Directory of Sites Related to Psychology. Some of their resources include database/archives, electronic journals/newsletters, grant and job information, general psychology/ medical links, reference materials, self-help, and software for psychology.

Brief History of Web Experimenting

`http://www.psychologie.uni-bonn.de/sozial/forsch/`
`birnbaum.htm`

A nicely put together review on how the Web has been used by psychologists to collect research data. The site also links you to a number of these research projects.

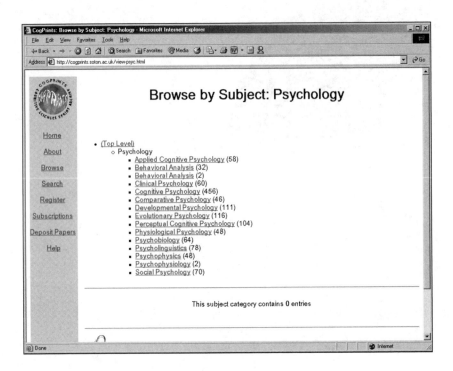

CogPrints

`http://cogprints.soton.ac.uk/view-psyc.html`

CogPrints is an electronic archive for papers in any area of Psychology, Neuroscience, and Linguistics, and many areas of Computer Science (e.g., artificial intelligence,robotics,vision, learning,speech,neural networks), Philosophy (e.g., mind, language,knowledge,science,logic), and Biology. Fulltext articles are available at this site.

Glossary of Online Psychiatry

`http://www.priory.com/gloss.htm`

Alphabetical list of hundreds of psychological/psychiatric terms and their definitions.

Psychwatch

`http://www.psychwatch.com/index.htm`

Psychwatch is a weekly email newsletter detailing events and Internet-related developments in the mental health field. You can have their newsletter emailed to you weekly. This is a fairly effortless way to keep with what is going on in mental health.

iSearch: Psychology

A Guide to Psychology and Its Practice

http://members.aol.com/avpsyrich/

This site provides a very extensive array of information about the practice or application of psychology, including information about insurance to opening a practice.

Irvine Health Foundation Lecture Series

http://www.ihf.org/

This site provides full-text articles from some of the most renowned psychologists in the world.

Psychology Departments on the Web

http://www.psychwww.com/resource/deptlist.htm

This very extensive listing of all psychology departments on the Internet is a must for any student making decision about which program to attend.

Careers in Psychology

http://www.psychwww.com/careers/index.htm

The resources on this page focus on: (1) careers in psychology at the bachelor's, master's, and doctoral level and (2) academic information about psychology at the bachelor's and graduate levels.

Ethics in Research

http://methods.fullerton.edu/chapter3.html

This site contains ethics codes and research links on the Internet.

Gallup Polls

http://www.gallup.com/

This site features public releases, special reports on key social and business-related issues, and Gallup Polls, a major source for public opinion data since 1935.

Educational Testing Service

http://www.ets.org/

This is the Educational Testing Service home page, with information for parents and students, educator-researchers and policymakers.

iSearch: Psychology

Code of Conduct

http://www.apa.org/ethics/code.html

This American Psychological Association site deals with ethical principles of psychologists and defines the code of conduct.

Statistics on the Web

http://www.spss.com

Statistics on the World Wide Web may be found at this site.

The Lifschitz Psychology Museum

http://www.netaxs.com/people/aca3/LPM.HTM

This is the World's First Virtual Museum of Psychology, established February 1, 1996.

Mind and Body

http://serendip.brynmawr.edu/Mind/Table.html

This site was derived for the Exhibition of Books from the Collections of the National Library of Medicine, held in honor of the Centennial Celebration of the American Psychological Association, August 7 to December 15, 1992

Statistic Glossary

http://www.cas.lancs.ac.uk/glossary_v1.1/main.html

This comprehensive site defines and gives examples of statistical concepts and terms.

William James

http://serendip.brynmawr.edu/Mind/James.html

This site contains a history of William James, the man who helped advance the Mind/Body Problem and the psychologist considered by many to be one of the most influential in history.

Psychological Research on the Net

http://psych.hanover.edu/APS/exponnet.html

Links to known experiments on the Internet that are psychologically related are organized by general topic areas with the topic areas listed alphabetically.

iSearch: Psychology

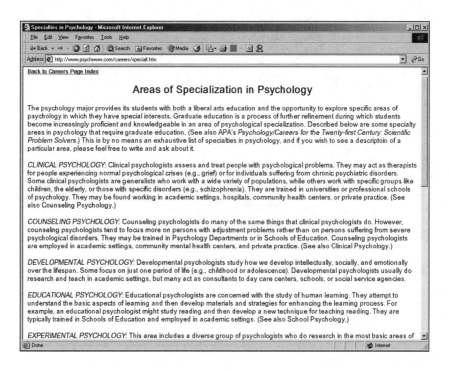

The screenshot shows a Microsoft Internet Explorer window titled "Specialties in Psychology" with the address http://www.psychwww.com/careers/specialt.htm displaying the following content:

Back to Careers Page Index

Areas of Specialization in Psychology

The psychology major provides its students with both a liberal arts education and the opportunity to explore specific areas of psychology in which they have special interests. Graduate education is a process of further refinement during which students become increasingly proficient and knowledgeable in an area of psychological specialization. Described below are some specialty areas in psychology that require graduate education. (See also APA's *Psychology/Careers for the Twenty-first Century: Scientific Problem Solvers.*) This is by no means an exhaustive list of specialties in psychology, and if you wish to see a descriptoin of a particular area, please feel free to write and ask about it.

CLINICAL PSYCHOLOGY: Clinical psychologists assess and treat people with psychological problems. They may act as therapists for people experiencing normal psychological crises (e.g., grief) or for individuals suffering from chronic psychiatric disorders. Some clinical psychologists are generalists who work with a wide variety of populations, while others work with specific groups like children, the elderly, or those with specific disorders (e.g., schizophrenia). They are trained in universities or professional schools of psychology. They may be found working in academic settings, hospitals, community health centers, or private practice. (See also Counseling Psychology.)

COUNSELING PSYCHOLOGY: Counseling psychologists do many of the same things that clinical psychologists do. However, counseling psychologists tend to focus more on persons with adjustment problems rather than on persons suffering from severe psychological disorders. They may be trained in Psychology Departments or in Schools of Education. Counseling psychologists are employed in academic settings, community mental health centers, and private practice. (See also Clinical Psychology.)

DEVELOPMENTAL PSYCHOLOGY: Developmental psychologists study how we develop intellectually, socially, and emotionally over the lifespan. Some focus on just one period of life (e.g., childhood or adolescence). Developmental psychologists usually do research and teach in academic settings, but many act as consultants to day care centers, schools, or social service agencies.

EDUCATIONAL PSYCHOLOGY: Educational psychologists are concerned with the study of human learning. They attempt to understand the basic aspects of learning and then develop materials and strategies for enhancing the learning process. For example, an educational psychologist might study reading and then develop a new technique for teaching reading. They are typically trained in Schools of Education and employed in academic settings. (See also School Psychology.)

EXPERIMENTAL PSYCHOLOGY: This area includes a diverse group of psychologists who do research in the most basic areas of

iSearch: Psychology

Major Areas of Psychology

http://www.psychwww.com/careers/specialt.htm

Explanations of ten different specialty areas in psychology—clinical, counseling, developmental, educational, experimental, health, industrial/organizational, physiological, school, and social psychology—are found at this site.

Experimental Psychology

http://www.york.ac.uk/depts/psych/www/etc/whatispsych.html

A description of experimental psychology, this site also deals with the common misconceptions of psychology.

Careers in Psychology

http://www.rider.edu/users/suler/gradschl.html

This site offers a detailed discussion of what one can do with a degree in psychology, the types of subfields, and how to get into graduate school.

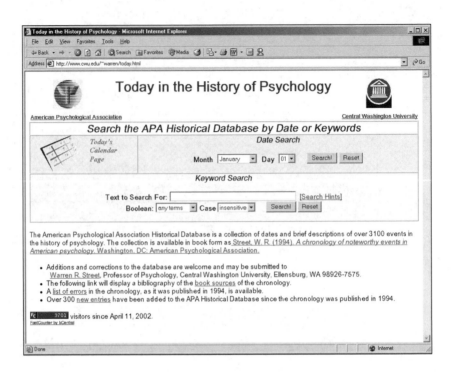

Today in the History of Psychology

http://www.cwu.edu/~warren/today.html

This interactive site allows the user to pick a date and see what happened in psychology on that date.

Usenet Newsgroups

http://www-psych.stanford.edu/cogsci/usenet.html

This is a large set of links to news groups.

Biological Psychology

A Primer of Imaging in Psychiatry

http://www.musc.edu/psychiatry/fnrd/primer_index.htm

A tutorial on how various imaging techniques, like fMRI, PET, and CT scans, have been used to examine brain-behavior relationships.

Brian Injury Guide

http://www.vh.org/Patients/IHB/Neuro/BrainInjury/
00TableOfContents.html

This site is provided by the Virtual Hospital and explains the consequences, diagnosis, and treatment of brain injury.

Two Brains are Better than One

http://whyfiles.org/026fear/physio1.html

The NSF claims that we have a second information processing system located around our stomachs! This article and its links provide evidence suggesting that our enteric system (i.e., gut) is capable of "thinking".

Neuroscience Tutorial

http://thalamus.wustl.edu/course/

The Neuroscience Tutorial from the Washington University School of Medicine provides an illustrated guide to the essential basics of clinical neuroscience created in conjunction with the first-year course for medical students.

Drugs, Brains, and Behavior

http://www.rci.rutgers.edu/~lwh/drugs/

Timmons & Hamilton provide a complete online textbook on psychopharmacology. In addition to the text, there are other valuable resources like a complete bibliography, definitions, and links to other resources.

Virtual Hospital: The Human Brain

http://www.vh.org/Providers/Textbooks/BrainAnatomy/
BrainAnatomy.html

The Department of Anatomy and Cell Biology at the University of Iowa designed this very user friendly and informative site about brain function and pathology (i.e., disease). "This electronic publication is intended to serve students of all the health and biological sciences who are seeking to understand the organization and functions of the human nervous system." The site provides some truly incredible images and explanations of the brain.

Basic Neural Processes Tutorials

http://psych.hanover.edu/Krantz/neurotut.html

This is a short tutorial of the basics of neural processing.

Neuropsychology Central

http://www.neuropsychologycentral.com/

An extremely large and diverse site that contains links to many other sites, including assessment, treatment, organizations, image sites and medical consideration, this is one of the most complete sites on the Net. It even includes music.

Neurotransmission

http://www.csuchico.edu/psy/BioPsych/
neurotransmission.html

A tutorial of the basics of neurotransmission, including the synapse and parts of the neuron can be accessed at this site.

Brain Imaging

http://www.bic.mni.mcgill.ca/demos/

These are interesting examples of brain imaging techniques. The brain imaging demos at this site require a graphics browser.

Neuroscience

http://faculty.washington.edu/chudler/ehceduc.html

This extremely detailed site consists of links for education and is large enough to spend several days exploring. It is must for anyone interested in the neuroscience.

Genetics

http://www.med.jhu.edu/Greenberg.Center/tutorial.htm

This site offers a rather in-depth discussion of genetics and inheritance.

The Whole Brain Atlas

http://www.med.harvard.edu/AANLIB/home.html

A complete reference to the brain, this site has information, images, and QuickTime movies all related to the brain. Included is a discussion on the pathology of Alzheimer's disease.

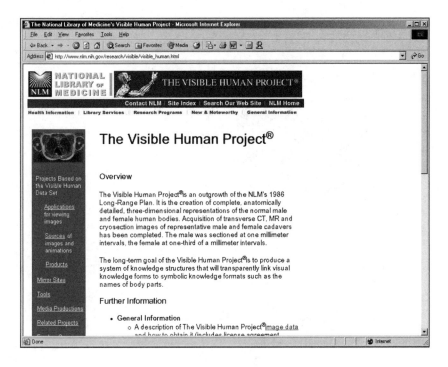

The Visible Human Project

http://www.nlm.nih.gov/research/visible/
visible_human.html

The Visible Human Project is creating complete, anatomically detailed, three-dimensional representations of the male and female human bodies.

Human Genome Project

http://www.ornl.gov/TechResources/Human_Genome/
home.html

This home page is maintained by the Human Genome Management Information System (HGMIS) for the U.S. Department of Energy Human Genome Program. Explore this site for material about the history, progress, research, and resources of the Human Genome Project.

Neuroscience

http://neuro.med.cornell.edu/VL/

This World Wide Web Virtual Library is supported by The Department of Neurology and Neuroscience at Cornell University Medical College.

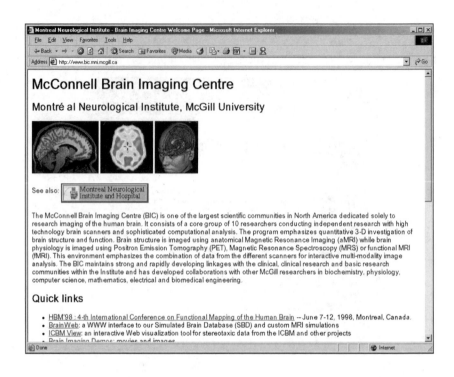

McConnell Brain Imaging Center

http://www.bic.mni.mcgill.ca/

The McConnell Brain Imaging Center (BIC) is one of the largest scientific communities in North America dedicated solely to research imaging of the human brain.

Splitting the Human Brain

http://ezinfo.ucs.indiana.edu/~pietsch/
split-brain.html

Detailed discussion of the split brain operations and its effects are presented from a research view point.

Sensation and Perception

Hearing and Balance Disorders

http://depts.washington.edu/otoweb/ear_anatomy.html

The Department of Otolaryngology-Head and Neck Surgery from the University of Washington provides a tour of the human ear along with descriptions and images of various conditions.

Brain Briefings: Pheromones

http://www.sfn.org/briefings/pheromones.html

This site is provided by the Society for Neuroscience and explains human pheromone perception.

HyperPhysics: Light and Vision

http://hyperphysics.phy-astr.gsu.edu/hbase/hframe.html

Georgia State University, Department of Physics, has developed a very detailed account of how our visual system responds to light energy. This site covers many sophisticated concepts like optics, propagation of light, quantum properties, etc.

Visual Illusions and Illustrations

http://dogfeathers.com/java/necker.html

This highly visual and interactive site provides examples of several visual illusions (e.g., the necker cube and the Fechner color illusion) as well as illustrates a couple of visual perception phenomenon (e.g., stereoscopic animated hypercube).

Eye Anatomy

http://www.stlukeseye.com/anatomy.htm

St. Luke's Cataract & Laser Institute has a lot of resources on their site related to visual anatomy and disease.

Kinesthetic Child

http://www.latitudes.org/learn01.html

The Fine Line Between ADHD and Kinesthetic Learners is discussed at this site.

Subliminal Persuasion

http://www.yahoo.com/Science/Cognitive_Science/Unconscious_Cognition/Subliminal_Perception/

A discussion of backward masking, hypnosis, and subliminal advertising can be found at this site.

iSearch: Psychology

Exploratorium

`http://www.exploratorium.edu/imagery/exhibits.html`

This site contains digital versions of Exploratorium exhibits. It is important understand that these versions in most cases are not adequate replacements for the real experiences that you will have if you are able to visit the Exploratorium in San Francisco. Most of these exhibits are electronic versions from the museum floor; a few are unique.

Historical Origins of Color Vision Research

`http://kiptron.psyc.virginia.edu/steve_boker/`
`ColorVision2/node3.html`

This site contains links to important individuals in the history of color vision research.

Illusionworks

`http://www.illusionworks.com/`

This is one the most comprehensive collections of optical and sensory illusions on the Internet.

Kubovy Perception Lab University of Virginia Department of Psychology

`http://minerva.acc.virginia.edu/~mklab/`

This site is a working laboratory studying topics like Gestalt detection, symmetry perception, picture perception, skin reading, and rhythm and time perception.

University of California at Santa Cruz Perceptual Science Laboratory

`http://mambo.ucsc.edu/`

The Perceptual Science Laboratory is engaged in a variety of experimental and theoretical inquiries in perception and cognition. A major research area concerns speech perception by ear, eye, and facial animation.

Vision Research WWW Servers

`http://www.socsci.uci.edu/cogsci/vision.html`

All there is to know about visual perception is contained in these links, from university laboratories to organizations concerned with visual perception.

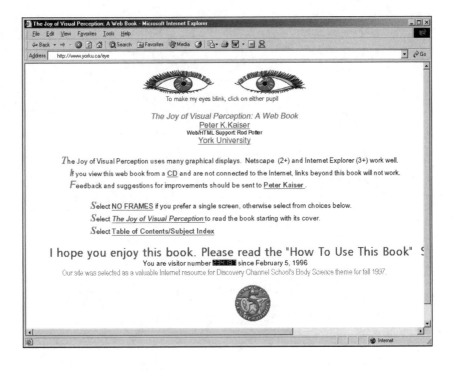

The Joy of Visual Perception: A Web Book

http://www.yorku.ca/eye/

This is an interactive book with links.

International Symposium on Olfaction and Taste

http://www.psychology.sdsu.edu/ISOT/

Details of a convention on olfaction and taste can be found at this site.

Cow Eye Dissection

http://www.exploratorium.edu/learning_studio/
cow_eye/index.html

This site offers a complete lab on cow eye dissection.

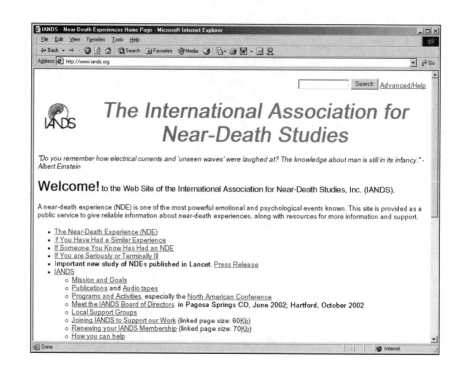

States of Consciousness

Near Death Experiences

http://www.iands.org/

This site, provided by the International Association for Near-Death Studies, Inc., is concerned with near-death experiences (NDE). The NDA states that such experiences are some of the most powerful emotional and psychological events known. This site is provided as a public service to give reliable information about near-death experiences, along with resources for more information and support.

New Clues to Why We Dream

http://www.psychoanalysis.org.uk/dreaming.htm

An article on dreaming by from the British Psychoanalytic Society. The article addresses the science of dreaming both in terms of the historical perspective (i.e., Freud) and the current perspective (i.e., neurophysiological).

Introduction to Club Drugs

http://www.nida.nih.gov/DrugPages/Clubdrugs.html

Clubs Drugs presented by this site include Alcohol, LSD (Acid), MDMA (Ecstasy), GHB, GBL, Ketamine (Special-K), Fentanyl, Rohypnol, amphetamines and methamphetamine. Information concerning their toxicity, street names, and primary euphoric effects are addressed.

Scientific Approaches to Consciousness: Reductionism Debated

`http://www.nimh.nih.gov/events/conscvideo.cfm`

The National Institute for Mental Health (NIMH) has made a debate concerning consciousness available to the public through RealPlayer. Some of the most influential scientists in the area of consciousness present their findings and debate with their peers.

What is Sleep . . . and why do we do it?

`http://faculty.washington.edu/chudler/sleep.html`

This site provides a basic overview of sleep, how it is measured, and what it is thought to accomplish.

Association for the Scientific Study of Consciousness

`http://assc.caltech.edu/`

"ASSC promotes research within cognitive science, neuroscience, philosophy, and other relevant disciplines in the sciences and humanities, directed toward understanding the nature, function, and underlying mechanisms of consciousness."

A Primer of Drug Actions

`http://www.addictionscience.net/ASNprimer.htm`

An online text on the nature of drug addiction, the biological basis of addiction, brain reward systems, drug classification, experimental methods, and links to other drug addiction resources.

Sleep Disorders

`http://www.sleepnet.com/disorder.htm`

All of the common sleep disorders are discussed at this site.

Dreams

`http://www.dreamgate.com/dream/resources/online97.htm`

A massive site that contains Mail List, Usenet Newsgroups, and Web sites by Category: Dream Sharing, Magazines and Journals, Information, Education

iSearch: Psychology

and Organizations, Personal Dream Journals, Religion, Spirituality and Healing (and Shamanism), Lucid Dreaming, Psi, Paranormal, Telepathic Dreaming, Dream Science and Research, Dreams and Anthropology, Dream Bibliography Collections, Dream Art, Dream Software, Jung and Dreams, Freud and Dreams, Books and Articles Online, and Lists of Links.

World Sleep Home Pages

http://bisleep.medsch.ucla.edu/

The Sleep home pages provide a comprehensive resource for individuals who are involved in the research or treatment of sleep and sleep-related disorders.

Substance Use and Abuse

http://orion.it.luc.edu/~pcrowe/375link.htm

Links from a course at Loyola University taught on addiction/substance abuse are found at this site. It includes many diverse links from varying view points on this state of consciousness.

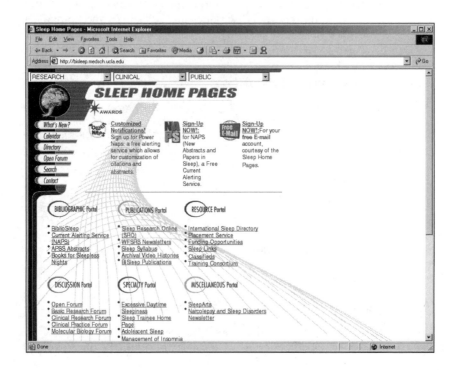

iSearch: Psychology

Memory and Learning

Interactive Classical Conditioning

`http://www.uwm.edu/~johnchay/cc.htm`

This site provides an interactive module that illustrates the basic concepts of Pavlovian conditioning.

Interactive Operant Conditioning

`http://www.uwm.edu/~johnchay/oc.htm`

This site provides a very informative and highly graphical description of operant conditioning.

Overview of Operant Conditioning

`http://epsych.msstate.edu/adaptive/Fuzz/index.html`

This site has an interactive program for operant conditioning and shaping. It may be useful for students new to the area of operant conditioning.

Short-term Memory

`http://olias.arc.nasa.gov/cognition/tutorials/`
`STM/index.html`

This site, sponsored by NASA, has several interesting and interactive tests concerning short-term memory

Glossary of Conditioning Terms

`http://www.psychology.uiowa.edu/Faculty/`
`Wasserman/Glossary/index%20set.html`

This is an interactive glossary of terms most often used in learning courses.

Working Memory and the Brain

`http://www.sciam.com/0897issue/0897trends.html`

Scientific American presents an article about functional imaging techniques and working memory. "Studies of the brains of monkeys and, more recently, of humans are revealing the neural underpinnings of working memory, one of the mind's most crucial functions."

Behavior Analysis Listservs

`http://www.coedu.usf.edu/behavior/listserv.html`

This is a listserv.

iSearch: Psychology

Common Cents

http://www.exploratorium.edu/memory/index.html

This site presents experiments in memory from the Exploratorium in San Francisco on memory for United States pennies.

Cognitive Learning

http://bobcat.oursc.k12.ar.us/~jdharris/cogmem.html

A text only discussion of cognitive learning can be found at this site.

Structures in Memory

http://www.ils.nwu.edu/e-for-e/nodes/NODE-8-pg.html

This site attempts to understand the variety of structures we have in our memories. There are many links to help define the discussion of structures of memory.

Positive Reinforcement: Overview of Behavioral Psychology

http://chiron.valdosta.edu/whuitt/col/behsys/
behsys.html

This site discusses theories and defines terms in the behavioral perspective of learning.

Classical Conditioning

http://www.indiana.edu/~iuepsyc/P103/lear/lear.html

Examples and demonstrations of classical and operant conditioning are found at this site.

Cognition and Intelligence

Top 100 Works in Cognitive Psychology

http://cogsci.umn.edu/millennium/final.html

A collection of some of the most important works/publications in the area of cognitive psychology.

The Cognitive Basis of Gender Stereotypes

http://www.psichi.org/content/publications/
eye/volume/vol_3/3_2/matlin.asp

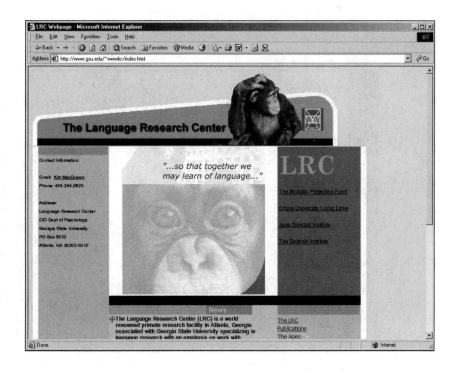

iSearch: Psychology

An article presented by Psi Chi, the National Honor Society for Psychology, addressing some of the cognitive mechanisms involved in creating and maintaining gender stereotypes.

Can Animals Use Language

`http://www.gsu.edu/~wwwlrc/index.html`

The Language Research Center (LRC) is a world renown primate research facility in Atlanta, Georgia, associated with Georgia State University specializing in language research with an emphasis on work with bonobos (Pan paniscus) and chimpanzees (Pan troglodytes).

Artificial Intelligence: Pros and Cons

`http://library.thinkquest.org/18242/ai_phil.shtml`

It is a very interesting and informative site about artificial intelligence from both a philosophical and practical standpoint. It has a variety of interviews, examples, and articles that could be of interest to students interested in cognitive neuroscience.

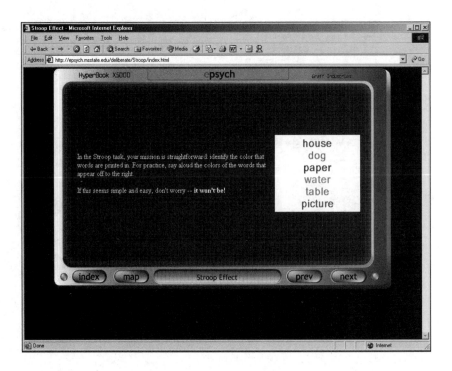

The Stroop Effect

http://epsych.msstate.edu/deliberate/Stroop/
index.html

The site noted above is an excellent site that provides mini-experiments and learning modules for students. This particular site provides a demonstration of the Stroop-effect.

The General Intelligence Factor

http://www.sciam.com/specialissues/1198intelligence/
1198gottfred.html

"Also known as g, the general intelligence factor is what IQ tests are all about. Despite the political controversy surrounding it, the test scores and their differences, the author argues, are meaningful indicators not only of academic performance but also of future life outcomes, such as employment, divorce and poverty."

Language Problems: Aphasia

http://www.aphasia.org/

The National Aphasia Association is a nonprofit organization that promotes public education, research, rehabilitation, and support services to assist people with aphasia and their families.

The Center for Neural Basis of Cognition

`http://www.cnbc.cmu.edu/`

Many links to other sites on science of cognition may be found at this site.

Literature, Cognition, and the Brain

`http://www2.bc.edu/~richarad/lcb/home.html`

This Web page features research at the intersection of literary studies, cognitive theory, and neuroscience.

Brain and Cognition Journal

`http://www.apnet.com/www/journal/br.htm`

A journal of clinical, experimental, and theoretical research, this site publishes original research articles, theoretical papers, critical reviews, case histories, historical articles, and scholarly notes.

IQ Tests

`http://www.2h.com/Tests/iqtrad.phtml`

Large number of IQ tests, puzzles, and practice items all in the area of intelligence testing may be found at this site.

Test of Intelligence

`http://www.geocities.com/CapitolHill/1641/iqown.html`

This site offers a traditional test of intelligence, with answers provided.

Cognitive Psychology

`http://www.haverford.edu/psych/CogPsycpage.html`

Cognitive Psychology Resources on the Web is sponsored by Haverford College, and includes many demonstrations and experiments.

Artificial Intelligence Subject Index

`http://ai.iit.nrc.ca/misc.html`

This extremely large site has links to all phases of artificial intelligence, including newsgroups, other sites bibliographies and data bases.

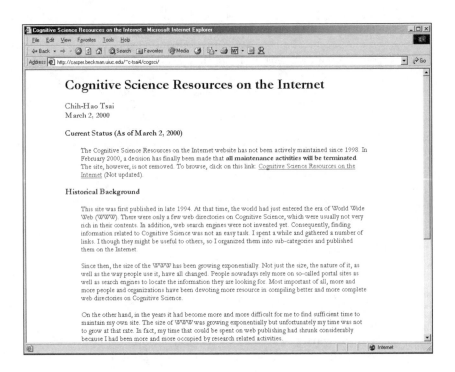

Cognitive Science Resources on the Internet

http://casper.beckman.uiuc.edu/~c-tsai4/cogsci/

Cognitive science is the study of intelligence and intelligent systems. This site has many links to help define this area of study.

Braintainment Center

http://www.brain.com/

This is a large and interesting page that contains several activities centered around the theme of studying and enhancing intelligence. This site is famous for the five minute IQ test.

Creativity Web

http://www.ozemail.com.au/~caveman/Creative/

Resources for creativity and innovation may be found at this site.

The Intelligence Page

http://www.euthenasia.org/mensal.html

Many international links on intelligence, including many international Mensa links may be found at this site.

Cognitive Learning

`http://bobcat.oursc.k12.ar.us/~jdharris/cogmem.html`

This site offers a text-only discussion of cognitive learning.

Motivation and Emotion

Introduction to Motivation and Emotion

`http://www.nimh.nih.gov/publicat/baschap1.cfm`

A thorough introduction to the field of motivation and emotion from the National Institute of Mental Health.

Jealousy Self Assessment

`http://www.psychtests.com/tests/alltests.html`

This site provides several interactive tests on jealousy. It might be interesting to compare the results across gender, although it shouldn't be taken too seriously. This test might serve as a good critical thinking exercise for students.

National Gambling Impact Study Commission

`http://www.ngisc.gov/`

Information regarding the social, psychological, and financial impact of gambling in America.

Genderbender

`http://www.utdallas.edu/~waligore/digital/garvey.html`

This site provides and interactive test on one's perception of their own sex roles. It is based on the Bem sex role inventory. It should be an interesting way to get a discussion started on sex-typing and stereotypes.

Measuring Emotional Quotients

`http://eqi.org/`

The information on this site is organized into two basic groups: Academic—A resource for those interested in serious scientific and academic research in the field of emotions and emotional intelligence. Everything else—Contains practical information on what I call EQ, which I define as the development of one's innate emotional intelligence. Also contains a variety of personal growth and related writings and resources.

Motivation

```
http://choo.fis.utoronto.ca/FIS/Courses/LIS1230/
LIS1230sharma/motive4.htm
```

A discussion of several theories of motivation may be found at this site.

Go Ask Alice

```
http://www.goaskalice.columbia.edu/
```

This site offers discussions of real life sexual motivations.

Anger

```
http://www.apa.org/pubinfo/anger.html
```

Anger is an emotional state that varies in intensity from mild irritation to intense fury and rage. Like other emotions, it is accompanied by physiological and biological changes. This site explores the varied aspects of the emotion anger.

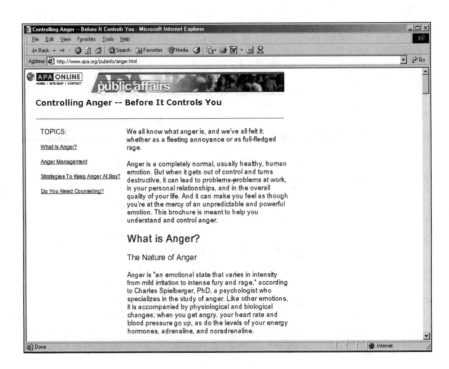

Abraham Maslow

`http://sol.brunel.ac.uk/~jarvis/bola/motivation/`
`masmodel.html`

Abraham Maslow Need-Satisfaction Model of Motivation is discussed at this site. Maslow is one of the major figures in the study on need-satisfaction in this century.

Child and Adolescent Development

The Visible Embryo

`http://www.visembryo.com/`

The Visible Embryo is a comprehensive resource of information on human development from conception to birth, designed for both medical student and interested lay people. This site offers a detailed pictorial account of normal and abnormal development.

Fetal Development

`http://www.w-cpc.org/fetal.html`

This site provides a systematic overview of fetal development along with numerous pictures.

Fetal Psychology

`http://www.leaderu.com/orgs/tul/psychtoday9809.html`

This article presents some very interesting findings in the area of fetal psychology.

Attention Deficit Disorder

`http://www.ncpamd.com/adhd.htm`

This site provides an extensive list of resources related to the diagnosis, prognosis, and treatment of ADHD.

Learning Disabilities: Dyslexia

`http://www.interdys.org/`

The International Dyslexia Association is an international, non-profit organization dedicated to the study and treatment of the learning disability, dyslexia. The IDA was established to continue the pioneering work of Dr. Samuel T. Orton, a neurologist who was one of the firsts to begin to identify dyslexia and develop effective teaching approaches.

iSearch: Psychology

Dyslexia Center

http://www.dyslexiacenter.com/

This is another site dedicated to understanding dyslexia.

America Reads

http://www.ed.gov/inits/americareads/nichd.html

The America Reads Challenge recognizes the supreme importance of an early and successful start to learning to read. Providing children with the right literacy and reading experiences in the early years is likely to set the stage for successful reading and citizenship in later years. To determine the literacy, language, and reading experiences that are important for young readers, we rely on the substantial research that has been conducted in beginning reading by researchers all over the world, and particularly by researchers at Federally sponsored agencies in the United States.

Whole-Language versus Phonics

http://www.education-world.com/a_curr/curr029.shtml

Whole Language and Phonics: Can They Work Together? This site provides an article addressing the debate between whole-language and phonics.

Reading Instruction

http://www.tampareads.com/phonics/phonics-articles.htm

Index to articles on two different reading methods—click link to see article.

Erikson's Eight Stages of Psychosexual Development

http://snycorva.cortland.edu/~ANDERSMO/ERIK/welcome.HTML

This site consists of a discussion of Erikson's stages of psychosocial development.

Adolescent Development

http://www.yale.edu/ynhti/curriculum/units/1991/5/91.05.07.x.html

This site discusses the physiological and psychological development of the adolescent.

Pregnancy and Early Care

http://www.parentsplace.com/pregnancy

This extensive site includes many discussions and links on the topics of pregnancy and early care for infants.

Young Children

http://www.earlychildhood.com/

The source of information for all who share an interest in improving the education and general life experience of young children, this is a place for getting advice from experts in the early childhood field, expanding your collection of creative projects, and sharing ideas and questions with the early childhood community.

Classic Theories of Child Development

http://childstudy.net/cdw.html

This large site includes tutorials on theory (a discussion of the classic theories of child development), and a key word search engine.

iSearch: Psychology

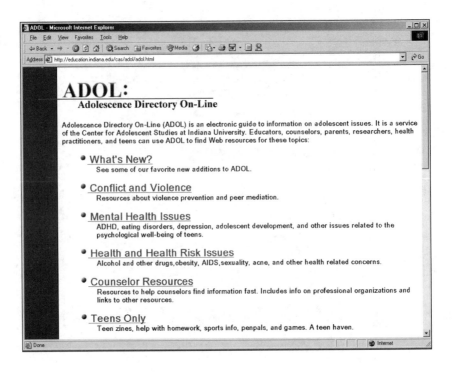

Adolescence Directory Online

`http://education.indiana.edu/cas/adol/adol.html`

Adolescence Directory Online (ADOL) is an electronic guide to information on adolescent issues. It is a service of the Center for Adolescent Studies at Indiana University for use by educators, counselors, parents, researchers, health, practitioners, and teens.

The Parent's Page

`http://www.moonlily.com/parents`

An extensive listing of traditional and nontraditional birthing, parenting, and pregnancy issues can be found at this site.

Midwifery, Pregnancy, Birth, and Breast-feeding

`http://www.moonlily.com/obc`

Links and articles on midwifery, pregnancy, birth, and breast-feeding are available at this site.

Adolescence: Change and Continuity

http://www.personal.psu.edu/faculty/n/x/
nxd10/adolesce.htm

This Web site provides an introduction to some of the developmental changes that shape our lives between puberty and the end of college. Although each life unfolds in its own unique pattern, this site provides information about the ways biological, psychological, and sociological influences systematically combine to shape its course.

Piaget

http://www.piaget.org/biography/biog.html

This site is a short biography of Jean Piaget.

Vygotsky on Development

http://rock.uwc.edu/psych/psy360/outlines/Cogearl.htm

Vygotsky's sociocultural view of development is covered at this site.

Language Development

http://www.parentingme.com/language.htm

This is a site dedicated to the understanding of language development.

Adult Development

National Center for Fathering

http://www.fathers.com/

This is a site dedicated to educating the public about the importance of fathers as well as providing practical resources for fathers.

The National Fatherhood Initiative

http://www.fatherhood.org/

The mission of the National Fatherhood Initiative (NFI) is to improve the well-being of children by increasing the number of children growing up with loving, committed and responsible fathers.

iSearch: Psychology

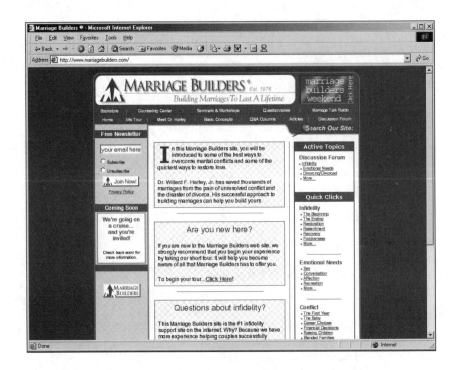

Marriage Builders

`http://www.marriagebuilders.com/`

In this Marriage Builders site, you will be introduced to some of the best ways to overcome marital conflicts and some of the quickest ways to restore love.

Journal of Family Psychology

`http://www.apa.org/journals/fam.html`

This APA sponsored journal on the family provides numerous full-text journals on issues relevant to families.

Mental and Physical Health Effects on Divorced People

`http://www.divorcereform.org/health.html`

Many resources and statistics concerning the influence of divorce on physical and mental health.

The Buck Institute on Aging

http://www.buckinstitute.org/

The mission at the Buck Institute, an independent, nonprofit research center, is to increase the healthy years of each individual's life through research and education on the aging process and age-associated diseases.

The Health and Retirement Study

http://www.umich.edu/~hrswww/

The main purpose of this site is to present survey data that will inform researchers and policymakers about elderly populations particularly concerning retirement.

Huffington Center on Aging

http://www.hcoa.org/

These pages will provide you with an overview of the research efforts, educational initiatives, and training programs of the center as well as affiliated clinical services and training activities administered by the center.

Human Nutrition Research Center on Aging

http://www.hnrc.tufts.edu/

The overall mission of the HNRC is to explore the relationship between nutrition and good health and to determine the nutritional and dietary requirements of the maturing and elderly population. The interaction between nutrition and the onset and progression of aging and associated degenerative conditions is of special concern.

National Institute on Aging (NIA)

http://www.nia.nih.gov

The National Institute on Aging (NIA) is one of the National Institutes of Health, the principal biomedical research agency of the United States Government. The NIA promotes healthy aging by conducting and supporting biomedical, social, and behavioral research and public education.

Adult Development

http://www.css.edu/depts/grad/nia/index.htm

Research training in the psychology of aging can be found at this site.

iSearch: Psychology

The Society for Research in Adult Development

http://www.norwich.edu/srad/index.html

The international membership of the Society for Research in Adult Development includes individuals from all disciplines who are interested in positive adult development.

Administration on Aging

http://www.aoa.dhhs.gov/

This Department of Health and Human Services site on the Administration on Aging offers extensive links to government services and other sites. It is a good site to explore the graying of America.

Personality

Early Childhood Behavior and Temperament Predict Later Substance Use

http://www.nida.nih.gov/NIDA_Notes/NNVOL10N1/
Earlychild.html

By the first grade, or earlier, children show temperament and behavior traits that are powerful indicators of their inclination to use and abuse drugs in their teenage and adult years. Researchers have identified not only common childhood risk factors and behaviors that predict drug abuse potential but also protective factors that shield some children from influences to use drugs.

Vulnerability and Resilience

http://www.nimh.nih.gov/publicat/baschap2.cfm

An intensive examination of the relationship between certain personality characteristics and their influence on vulnerability and resilience sponsored by the National Institute of Mental Health.

What Is a Personality/Social Psychologist?

http://www.spsp.org/what.htm

The Society for Personality and Social Psychology (SPSP) was founded in 1974 as Division 8 of the American Psychological Association. Today, SPSP includes both APA members and nonmembers in a wide array of subfields.

Encyclopedia of Mental Health: Shyness

http://www.shyness.com/encyclopedia.html

The Palo Alto Shyness Clinic provides a full-text review on the science of shyness. Topics like prevalence and diagnosis are covered, as are topics like the biology of shyness. The article is written by one of the foremost experts in the field of shyness.

Great Ideas in Personality

http://www.personalityresearch.org/

This Web site deals with scientific research programs in personality. They are offered as candidates for the title "great ideas"; whether they are indeed great remains an open question.

Major Personality Theorists

http://www.wynja.com/personality/theorists.html

This site includes many of the major personality theorists, with detailed material on their theories.

Personality

http://bill.psyc.anderson.edu/perth/freud.htm

Extensive links to major individuals and theories in the study of personality are available at this site.

Carl Rogers

http://psy1.clarion.edu/jms/Rogers.html

This site discusses Carl Rogers and his views on the therapeutic relationship.

Personality Tests

http://www.2h.com/Tests/personality.phtml

This site contain a large selection of personality tests that you can take on the Internet. Including test of anxiety, self esteem, attention deficient and type A personality.

Do You Have a Type A Personality?

http://www.queendom.com/tests/personality/
type_a_personality_access.html

An online personality test, containing seventeen items, which attempts to differentiate between A- and B-type personalities.

Classical Adlerian Psychology

http://ourworld.compuserve.com/homepages/
hstein/homepage.htm

Classical Adlerian psychology is a values-based, fully-integrated theory of personality, model of psychopathology, philosophy of living, strategy for preventative education, and techniques of psychotherapy.

FreudNet

http://www.nypsa.org

Linked sites dealing with the life's work of Freud, and his theories and contributions to psychology in the first half of this century.

The Keirsey Temperament Sorter

http://www.keirsey.com/cgi-bin/keirsey/newkts.cgi

The Keirsey Temperament Sorter by David Keirsey is a personality test which scores results according to the Myers-Briggs system (the actual Myers-Briggs test is a professional instrument and may only be administered by a licensed practitioner).

Stress and Health

Health Psychology and Rehabilitation

http://healthpsych.com/index.html

Research, viewpoints and practical suggestions about the practice of health psychology in medical and rehabilitation settings.

The Truth About Sexually Transmitted Diseases

http://www.unspeakable.com/

A frank, accurate, and unembarrassed guide to the prevention and treatment of sexually transmitted diseases sponsored by Pfizer Pharmaceuticals.

Stress Management: A Review of Principles

http://www.unl.edu/stress/mgmt

iSearch: Psychology

This document presents the core concepts of stress management education. It includes everything from defining stress to detailing the adverse consequences on one physical and mental state.

Health Risk Assessment

`http://www.youfirst.com/index.asp`

This questionnaire uses information provided by you regarding diet, exercise, stress, drug and alcohol usage, body size, blood pressure levels, and family history information to generate a health report. The health report is very comprehensive, personalized, and confidential. Throughout the personalized report, you are given your current health status on a number of variables, as well as information on your potential health status.

The American Institute on Stress

`http://www.stress.org/`

This site is dedicated to advancing the knowledge base in the role of stress in health and disease. This site also serves as a national clearinghouse on stress-related information.

Sidran Traumatic Stress Foundation

`http://www.sidran.org/`

Sidran Traumatic Stress Foundation is a nonprofit charitable organization devoted to education, advocacy, and research to benefit people who are suffering from injuries of traumatic stress.

Crises, Grief, and Healing

`http://www.webhealing.com/`

A site dedicated to helping people understand and recovery from strong emotional loss.

Go Ask Alice

`http://www.goaskalice.columbia.edu/`

This site contains the Health Education and Wellness program of the Columbia University Health Service. This site is committed to helping individuals make choices that will contribute to their personal health and happiness, and to the well-being of others.

iSearch: Psychology

The Longevity Game

http://www.northwesternmutual.com/games/longevity/

This game determines how long one can expect to live based on one's current life style. This site is also listed as an activity.

Social Anxiety Test

http://www.queendom.com/tests/health/
social_anxiety_r_access.html

An online social anxiety test containing twenty-five items is offered at this site.

What is Stress?

http://www.ivf.com/stress.html

This site describes stress as the "wear and tear" our bodies experience as we adjust to our continually changing environment; it has physical and emotional effects on us and can create positive or negative feelings. Techniques for stress management and reductions are discussed.

The Society of Behavioral Medicine

http://psychweb.syr.edu/sbm/sisterorg.html

Extensive links to psychology sources, government sources, and public health sites, including public health, psychology, and medicine can be found at this site.

The National Clearinghouse for Alcohol and Drug Information

http://www.health.org/

This site offers links to prevention and treatment of substance abuse. PREVLINE offers electronic access to searchable databases and substance abuse prevention materials that pertain to alcohol, tobacco, and drugs.

Abnormal Psychology

CounselingNet

http://www.counselingnet.com/

Online Counseling Psychology and Information For Anxiety, Depression, Stress, Relationships, Marriage, Addictions, Sexual Problems, Career and Personal Problems, Divorce, and Custody.

APA *DSM-IV* Diagnostic Classification

`http://www.behavenet.com/capsules/disorders/`
`dsm4classification.htm`

Near exhaustive listing of mental disorders grouped according to their *DSM-IV* classification.

The Center for Eating Disorders

`http://www.eating-disorders.com/`

Sponsored by St. Joseph Medical Center, this site provides information concerning the diagnosis, treatment, and medical consequences of eating disorders.

Internet Therapy

`http://www.metanoia.org/imhs/`

What is your opinion on psychologists conducting therapy or counseling online? "Now you can meet with a psychotherapist for private counseling or advice, from the privacy of your own computer. Using the Internet, professional counselors are forming effective helping relationships with people like you."

Drug and Alcohol Treatment and Prevention Global Network

`http://www.drugnet.net/metaview.htm`

Perhaps one of the most exhaustive sites on the Internet related to drug abuse and addiction. This site provides links to drug abuse and addiction resources all over the United States and world.

Mental Health InfoSource

`http://www.mhsource.com/`

This site is designed primarily for mental health professions. Numerous professional resources are located on this site. Additionally, there are links to specific psychological disorders, their cause, diagnosis, and treatment.

Center for the Study of Autism

`http://www.autism.org/`

The Center provides information about autism to parents and professionals, and conducts research on the efficacy of various therapeutic interventions.

iSearch: Psychology

Psychopharmacology Links

http://www.ncpamd.com/psychopharm.htm

Northern County Psychiatric Associates Psychiatric Services for Children, Adolescents, Adults and Families has assembled a comprehensive list of psychopharmacology resources. Most drug classes are included in this list as are numerous links to other psychopharmacology resources.

The Phobia List

http://phobialist.com

This site includes a complete listing of phobias.

Schizoid Personality Disorder

http://mentalhelp.net/disorders/sx30.htm

This site describes the symptoms of Schizoid personality disorder.

National Anxiety Foundation

http://lexington-on-line.com/naf.html

This site contains many links of the topic of anxiety disorders.

Bipolar Disorder

http://www.nimh.nih.gov/publicat/bipolarmenu.cfm

This is a site that offers a variety of links to information on bipolar disorder.

The Efficacy of Psychotherapy

http://www.apa.org/practice/peff.html

This site discusses the benefits of psychotherapy in 475 controlled studies, using only studies of patients seeking treatment for neuroses, true phobias, and emotional-somatic complaints. Statistical analysis of the data are discussed.

Behavior Therapy

http://site.health-center.com/brain/therapy/
default.htm

This site discusses how Behavior therapy focuses on what we do. This type of therapy works particularly well for problems in which certain maladaptive anxiety-causing behaviors recur such as phobias, anxiety disorders, obsessive-compulsive disorders, drug and alcohol problems, and eating disorders.

Interpersonal Therapy

http://site.health-center.com/brain/therapy/
default.htm

This site discusses Interpersonal therapy (IPT) which was developed for the treatment of depression. IPT has been empirically studied and has been shown, when used in conjunction with medication, to be superior to no active treatment and to medication alone.

Cognitive Therapy

http://site.health-center.com/brain/therapy/
default.htm

This site discusses how Cognitive psychotherapy focuses on identifying and changing negative thinking patterns. Often people with clinical depression make negative assumptions about their world. These assumptions lead them to have negative thoughts about themselves, their situation, and their future. These negative thoughts can create depressive feelings.

Internet Depression Resources List

http://www.blarg.net/~charlatn/Depression.html

This site includes links, discussion groups, help groups, and a comprehensive listing of site and resources on all types of mood disorders.

Eating Disorder

http://www.edap.org/

This home page provides some basic information about Eating Disorders, awareness, prevention, and eating disorders in general.

The Anxiety Panic Internet Resource

http://www.algy.com/anxiety/index.shtml

This site is for people interested in anxiety disorders such as panic attacks, phobias, shyness, generalized anxiety, obsessive-compulsive behavior and post-traumatic stress.

Sleep Disorders

http://www.sleepnet.com/disorder.htm

iSearch: Psychology

This site contains everything you wanted to know about sleep disorders but were too tired to ask.

Schizophrenia

`http://www.mentalhealth.com/dis/p20-ps01.html`

General information and links on schizophrenia, is available at this site, including description, research, and treatment.

Psychiatry Information for the General Public

`http://www.med.nyu.edu/Psych/public.html`

This site offers online testing and screening for disorders from NYU Department of Psychiatry Home Page.

Schizophrenia

`http://www.mentalhealth.com/book/p40-sc02.html`

This detailed site, produced by the British Columbia Friends of Schizophrenia Society, is one of the major reference sites on schizophrenia in the world.

BPD Central

`http://www.bpdcentral.com/`

Borderline Personality Disorder (BPD) is a major disorder in the personality disorders and anyone knowing someone so diagnosed should view this site, which offers listings of links for BPD.

Alzheimer's Disease

`http://www5.biostat.wustl.edu/alzheimer/`

The Alzheimer's Page is an educational service created and sponsored by the Washington University Alzheimer's Disease Research Center.

MentalHealth.Com

`http://www.mentalhealth.com/p.html`

Internet Mental Health, a free encyclopedia of mental health information. The goal of Internet Mental Health is to promote improved understanding, diagnosis, and treatment of mental illness throughout the world.

iSearch: Psychology

DSM *Criteria*

`http://www.apa.org/science/lib.html`

This extensive APA site consists of terms and definitions of *DSM* criteria and describes all of what is currently considered to be abnormal behavior by the American Psychiatric Association.

Two Views on Diagnostic Books

`http://www.apa.org/journals/nietzel.html`

This is an APA site that discusses of the pros and cons of the *DSM* series.

Social Psychology

Influence at Work: The Psychology of Persuasion

`http://www.influenceatwork.com/`

"Influence is a rapidly expanding field of psychological inquiry devoted to discovering the principles that determine beliefs, create attitudes, and move people to action. In other words, influence examines the process that causes humans to change."

Stanford Prison Experiment

`http://www.prisonexp.org/`

This site provides an overview of the now famous experiment by Philip G. Zimbardo entitled the "Stanford Prison Experiment." In addition to learning all about the experiment through various texts, this site also provides a slide tour describing the experiment and uncovering what it tells us about the nature of Human Nature.

Implicit Association Test

`http://buster.cs.yale.edu/implicit/`

This Web site presents a new method that demonstrates public-private and conscious-unconscious divergences much more convincingly than has been possible with previous methods. It also displays the method in a do-it-yourself demonstration form. This new method is called the Implicit Association Test, or IAT for short.

The Society of Experimental Social Psychology

`http://www.sesp.org/`

The Society of Experimental Social Psychology (SESP) is a scientific organization dedicated to the advancement of social psychology.

iSearch: Psychology

Cults and Psychological Manipulation

http://www.csj.org/

AFF, the leading professional organization concerned about cults and psychological manipulation, was founded 20 years ago in 1979. AFF is known for its professionalism, for building its practical educational services for families, former group members, helping professionals, educators, and young people on a base of scholarly study and research.

Social Research Methods

http://trochim.human.cornell.edu/index.html

This site is concerned with applied social research and evaluation. In addition to Bill Trochim's own work, you'll find lots of links to other locations on the Web that deal in applied social research methods.

Social Influence and Social Cognition

http://www.nimh.nih.gov/publicat/baschap5.cfm

This site, which is sponsored by the National Institute of Mental Health, reviews of some of the major issues in social psychology including Social influence, Social cognition, stereotyping and prejudice, social and personal identity, research directions, and a bibliography.

National Television Violence Study

http://www.reseau-medias.ca/eng/med/home/
resource/ntvs.htm

This study is the most elaborate and comprehensive assessment ever conducted of the context in which violence appears on TV.

Power of Persuasion in Art

http://wae.clever.net/webcat/powers/powers.htm

This online exhibit features eleven posters and one sound file from a more extensive exhibit that was presented in the National Archives Building in Washington, DC on persuasion.

Research on Conformity

http://www.science.wayne.edu/~wpoff/cor/grp/
conformt.html

Definitions and research on conformity are presented at this site.

The browser window shows:

"conformity"

the pressure to conform

return to "Influence"

key ideas
match
norms
group
size
ally

Conformity involves the changing of one's attitudes, opinions, or behaviors to **match** the attitudes, opinions, or behaviors of other people. This pressure to act like other people, sometimes despite our true feelings and desires, is a common everyday occurrence. This is do to the implied and spoken rules of the situation.

These "norms" tell us what we should or ought to be thinking, feeling, or doing if we want to fit in with a particular group. Most people **conform to norms** without much thinking about it. For example, most people tip in restaraunts, raise their hand when wishing to speak in a group setting, or sit down when they eat. While none of these incidences involve formal rules, most people comply with them. However, there are certain times when people are more or less likely to conform to the existing norms. Several factors affect the degree to which conformity will occur.

Group cohesiveness (the degree to which we are strongly attracted to a group and desire to maintain membership in it) increases the occurrance of conformity. For example, countless research studies exist which display the degree of conformity in sororities and fraternaties. In a like manner, the number of persons exerting pressure increases the amount of conformity.

This is true only to a certain point. A **group size** of about three to four people will exert pressure to conform. However, a larger group size does not increase the likelihood of conformity.

Finally, having an **ally** -- someone who disagrees with the majority-- results in much less conformity than when no social support exists for the target of conformity.

To report problems or ideas , e-mail us including the page name.

match
norms
group
size
ally

key

The Foot-in-the-Door

http://www.science.wayne.edu/~wpoff/cor/grp/
complian.html

Compliance and *The Foot-in-the-Door* tactic are detailed at this site.

Attraction and Love

http://www.telecom.csuhayward.edu/~psy3500/key03a.html

Different stages of attraction and love are described at this site.

National Civil Rights Museum

http://www.civilrightsmuseum.org

Reducing prejudice and discrimination is the goal of this site.

Locus of Control Test

http://www.queendom.com/tests/personality/
lc_access.html

This test assesses your locus of control orientation and your attributional style with forty-two items. A locus of control orientation is a belief about whether the outcomes of our actions are contingent on what we do (internal control orientation) or events outside our personal control (external control orientation).

Social Psychology Network

http://www.socialpsychology.org/

This page contains links to the major topics in social psychology. It is a very good starting place for any new student to the field of social psychology.

Jumping Off Place for Social Psychologists

http://swix.ch/clan/ks/CPSP1.htm#b_b

This site shows links to psychology-related resources available on the Internet. The links listed focus mostly on social psychology issues, but also consider other psychological topics such as clinical psychology.

Applied Psychology

School Psychology Resources for Psychologists, Parents, and Educators

http://www.bcpl.net/~sandyste/school_psych.html

Research learning disabilities, ADHD, functional behavioral assessment, autism, adolescence, parenting, psychological assessment, special education, mental retardation, mental health, and more.

Forensic Psychology

http://www.psychologyinfo.com/forensic

Forensic psychology is the interface between psychology and the law, so all psychological services provided for the legal community are forensic psychological services. Additionally, forensic psychologists provide services that are both clinical and forensic in nature, such as treating people how have witnessed a crime. This site provides an overview of the field and links to other sites.

International Society of Political Psychology

http://ispp.org/

The purpose of this site is to facilitate communication across disciplinary, geographic and political boundaries among scholars, concerned individuals in government and public posts, the communications media, and elsewhere who have a scientific interest in the relationship between politics and psychological processes.

Traffic Psychology

http://www.soc.hawaii.edu/leonj/leonj/leonpsy/
traffic/tpintro.html

Traffic psychology refers to the knowledge one acquires about how to use behavioral principles to modify one's own style of conduct in traffic situations including driving, bicycling, walking, and other forms of locomotion in shared spaces. A common activity in traffic psychology is to attempt to modify one's old driving persona to a new and better driving persona.

PsychLAW

http://www.psyclaw.org/

A site dedicated to the study of law and psychology. The American Psychological Association sponsors this site.

Psychology of Religion Pages

http://www.psywww.com/psyrelig/

This is a general introduction to the psychology of religion, for example, as scientists in Division 36 of the American Psychological Association study it. Here you will find a description of what psychologists have learned about how religion influences people's lives.

Sports Psychology

http://www.demon.co.uk/mindtool/page11.html

This is a massive page with many links in the area of sports psychology.

Human Factors and the FAA

http://www.hf.faa.gov/

This site provides the aviation community and other interested users with information about human factors research and applications under the auspices of the National Plan for Civil Aviation Human Factors

I/O

http://www.siop.org/Instruct/InGuide.htm

This detailed guide to the sub fields of industrial/organizational psychology.

iSearch: Psychology

I/O Survival Guide

`http://allserv.rug.ac.be/~flievens/guide.htm`

This guide provides a plethora of Internet sites valuable to the understanding of the field of industrial and organizational psychology.

Forensic Psychiatry

`http://ua1vm.ua.edu/~jhooper/`

Forensic psychiatry resource page contains links to other sites in the area.

Zeno's Forensic Page

`http://forensic.to/forensic.html`

This is a large site with many links in the area of forensic psychology.

CUErgo

`http://ergo.human.cornell.edu/`

Cornell's Human Factors and Ergonomics Program focuses on ways to improve comfort, performance, and health through the ergonomic design of products and environments.

Human Factors Home Page

`http://www.aviation.uiuc.edu/institute/acadProg/`
`epjp/humFacsites/hotlist.html`

This is a complete listing of interesting human factors sites maintained at University of Illinois at Urbana-Champaign.

Sports and Exercise Psychology

`http://spot.colorado.edu/~collinsj/`

This site includes listings of organizations, graduate programs, and mailing lists for sports and exercise psychology.

The Forensic Science Society

`http://www.forensic-science-society.org.uk`

This is the home page for the Forensic Science Society. The Forensic Science Society is interested in the origins of forensic science and careers in forensic science in the UK.

The Journal of Environmental Psychology

`http://www.apnet.com/www/journal/ps.htm`

The Journal of Environmental Psychology is directed toward individuals in a wide range of disciplines who have an interest in the study of the transactions and interrelationships between people and their sociophysical surroundings (including man-made and natural environments) and the relation of this field to other social and biological sciences and to the environmental professions.

Environmental Psychology

`http://www.snre.umich.edu/~rdeyoung/envtpsych.html`

This site offers an article on environmental psychology.

Human Factors at NASA

`http://human-factors.arc.nasa.gov/`

The NASA mission for this section is to develop a world-class center for human factors research, and to promote the broadest possible application of this research.

Other Online Resources

Allyn & Bacon Psychology Web Site

`www.ablongman.com/psychology`

This Web site provides an overview of Allyn and Bacon Psychology texts and their corresponding supplements. Web links provide content to review, enrich, and expand upon information in an accompanying Allyn and Bacon Psychology text.

Companion Web Sites

`http://www.abinteractive.com/gallery`

Our Companion Web sites use the Internet to provide you with various opportunities for further study and exploration. The CW offers study content and activities related to the text, as well as an interactive, online study guide. Quizzes containing multiple choice, true/false, and essay questions can be graded instantly, and forwarded to your instructor for recording—all online.

iSearch: Psychology

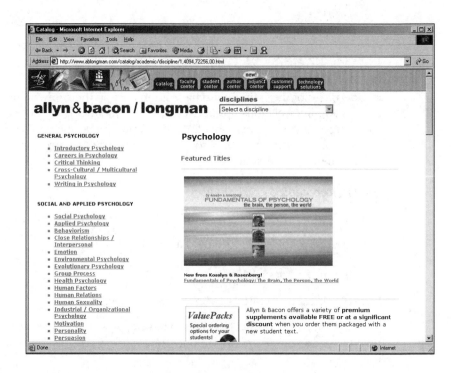

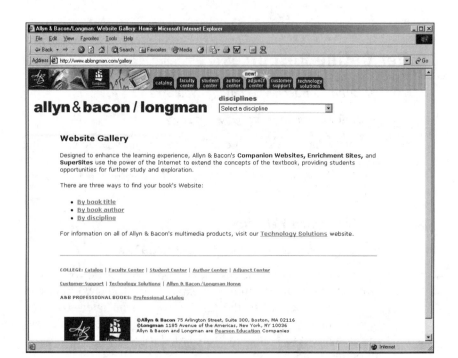

ContentSelect

What Is ContentSelect?

ContentSelect for Psychology

`http://www.ablongman.com/contentselect`

Allyn & Bacon and EBSCO Publishing, leaders in the development of electronic journal databases have exclusively collaborated to develop the Psychology ContentSelect Research Database, an online collection of leading scholarly and peer-reviewed journals in the discipline. Students can have unlimited access to a customized, searchable collection of discipline-specific articles from top-tier academic publications such as: *The Personality and Social Psychology Bulletin, The Journal of Social Psychology, Psychology, Evolution, and Gender, The Journal of Human Development,* and *Attachment and Human Development.*

In addition, new features are especially designed to help you with the research process:

- **Start Writing!** With detailed information on the process of writing a research paper, from finding a topic, to gathering data, using the library, using online sources, and more.

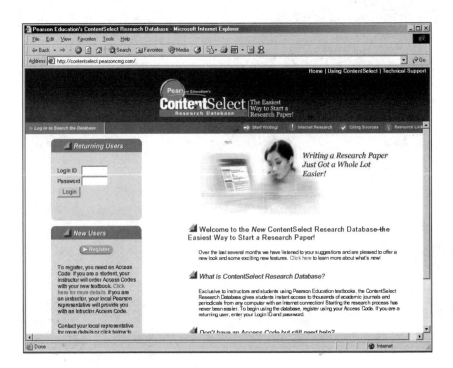

- **Internet Research** and **Resource Links** aggregates links to many of the best sites on the Web, providing more tips and best practices to help you use the Web for research.
- **Citing Sources.** Featuring excerpts from the best-selling book on research paper, this section helps you understand how and when to cite sources, and includes examples of various citation styles.

How to Use ContentSelect

To begin exploring the great resources available in the ContentSelect Research Database Web site:

Step 1: Go to: **http://www.ablongman.com/contentselect**

Step 2: The resources on the home page will help you start the research and writing process and cite your sources. For invaluable research help,

- Click **Citing Sources** to see how to cite materials with these citation styles: MLA, APA, CMS, and CBE.

iSearch: Psychology

- Click **Start Writing!** for step-by-step instructions to help you with the process of writing a research paper.

- Click **Resource Links** and **Internet Research** to link to many of the best sites on the Web with tips to help you efficiently use the Web for research.

Step 3: Register! To start using the ContentSelect Research Database, you will need to register using the access code and instructions located on the inside front cover of this guide. You only need to register once—after you register, you can return to ContentSelect at any time, and log in using your personal login name and password.

Step 4: Log in! Type in your login name and password in the spaces provided to access ContentSelect. Then click through the pages to enter the research database, and see the list of disciplines. You can search for articles within a single discipline, or select as many disciplines as you want! To see the list of journals included in any database, just click the "**complete title list**" link located next to each discipline—check back often, as this list will grow throughout the year!

Step 5: To begin your search, simply select your discipline(s), and **click "Enter"** to begin your search. For tips and detailed search instructions, please visit the "ContentSelect Search Tips" section included in this guide.

For more help, and search tips, click the Online Help button on the right side of your screen.

Go to **www.ablongman.com/contentselect** now, to discover the easiest way to start a research paper!

ContentSelect Search Tips

Searching for articles in ContentSelect is easy! Here are some tips to help you find articles for your research paper.

Tip 1: **Select a discipline.** When you first enter the ContentSelect Research Database, you will see a list of disciplines. To search within a single discipline, click the name of the discipline. To search in more than one discipline, click the box next to each discipline and click the **ENTER** button.

iSearch: Psychology

Basic Search

The following tips will help you with a Basic Search.

Tip 2: **Basic Search.** After you select your discipline(s), you will go to the Basic Search Window. Basic Search lets you search for articles using a variety of methods. You can select from: Standard Search, Match All Words, Match Any Words, or Match Exact Phrase. For more information on these options, click the Search Tips link at any time!

Tip 3: **Using AND, OR, and NOT** to help you search. In Standard Search, you can use AND, OR and NOT to create a very broad or very narrow search:

- **AND** searches for articles containing all of the words. For example, typing **education AND technology** will search for articles that contain **both** education AND technology.

- **OR** searches for articles that contains at least one of the terms. For example, searching for **education OR technology** will find articles that contain either education OR technology.

- **NOT** excludes words so that the articles will not include the word that follows "NOT." For example, searching for **education NOT technology** will find articles that contain the term education but NOT the term technology.

Tip 4: **Using Match All Words.** When you select the Match All Words option, you do not need to use the word AND—you will automatically search for articles that only contain all of the words. The order of the search words entered in does not matter. For example, typing **education technology** will search for articles that contain **both** education AND technology.

Tip 5: **Using Match Any Words.** After selecting the "Match Any Words" option, type words, a phrase, or a sentence in the window. ContentSelect will search for articles that contain any of the terms you typed (but will not search for words such as **in** and **the**). For example, type **rising medical costs in the United States** to find articles that contain *rising, medical, costs, United,* or *States.* To limit your search to find articles that contain exact terms, use *quotation marks*—for example, typing "United States" will only search for articles containing "United States."

Tip 6: **Using Match Exact Phrase.** Select this option to find articles containing an exact phrase. ContentSelect will search for articles that include all the words you entered, exactly as you entered them. For example, type **rising medical costs in the United**

States to find articles that contain the exact phrase "rising medical costs in the United States."

Guided Search

The following tips will help you with a Guided Search.

Tip 7: To switch to a Guided Search, click the **Guided Search** tab on the navigation bar, just under the EBSCO Host logo. The *Guided Search Window* helps you focus your search using multiple text boxes, Boolean operators (AND, OR, and NOT), and various search options.

To create a search:

- Type the words you want to search for in the Find field.

- Select a field from the drop-down list. For example: AU-Author will search for an author. For more information on fields, click Search Tips.

- Enter additional search terms in the text boxes (optional), and select *and, or, not* to connect multiple search terms (see Tip 3 for information on *and, or,* and *not*).

- Click **Search.**

Expert Search

The following tips will help you with an Expert Search.

Tip 8: To switch to an Expert Search, click the **Expert Search** tab on the navigation bar, just under the EBSCO Host logo. The *Expert Search Window* uses your keywords and search history search for articles. Please note, searches run from the Basic or Guided Search Windows are not saved to the History File used by the Expert Search Window—only Expert Searches are saved in the history.

Tip 9: Expert Searches use **Limiters** and **Field Codes** to help you search for articles. For more information on Limiters and Field Codes, click Search Tips.

Explore all the search options available in ContentSelect! For more information and tips, click the Online Help button, located on the right side of every page.

iSearch: Psychology

Glossary

Your Own Private Glossary

The Glossary in this book contains reference terms you'll find useful as you get started on the Internet. After a while, however, you'll find yourself running across abbreviations, acronyms, and buzzwords whose definitions will make more sense to you once you're no longer a novice (or "newbie"). That's the time to build a glossary of your own. For now, the Webopedia gives you a place to start.

alias A simple email address that can be used in place of a more complex one.

AVI Audio Video Interleave. A video compression standard developed for use with Microsoft Windows. Video clips on the World Wide Web are usually available in both AVI and QuickTime formats.

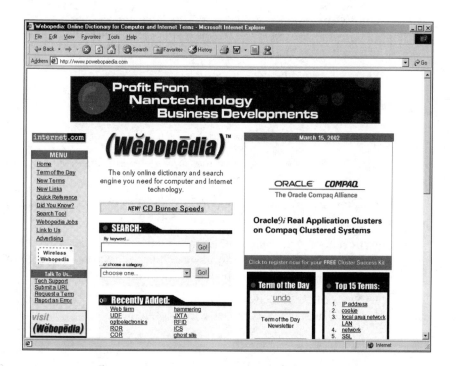

bandwidth Internet parlance for capacity to carry or transfer information such as email and Web pages.

browser The computer program that lets you view the contents of Web sites.

client A program that runs on your personal computer and supplies you with Internet services, such as getting your mail.

cyberspace The whole universe of information that is available from computer networks. The term was coined by science fiction writer William Gibson in his novel *Neuromancer,* published in 1984.

DNS See *domain name server.*

domain A group of computers administered as a single unit, typically belonging to a single organization such as a university or corporation.

domain name A name that identifies one or more computers belonging to a single domain. For example, "apple.com".

domain name server A computer that converts domain names into the numeric addresses used on the Internet.

download Copying a file from another computer to your computer over the Internet.

email Electronic mail.

emoticon A guide to the writer's feelings, represented by typed characters, such as the Smiley :-). Helps readers understand the emotions underlying a written message.

FAQs Frequently Asked Questions

flame A rude or derogatory message directed as a personal attack against an individual or group.

flame war An exchange of flames (see above).

ftp File Transfer Protocol, a method of moving files from one computer to another over the Internet.

home page A page on the World Wide Web that acts as a starting point for information about a person or organization.

hypertext Text that contains embedded *links* to other pages of text. Hypertext enables the reader to navigate between pages of related information by following links in the text.

LAN Local Area Network. A computer network that is located in a concentrated area, such as offices within a building.

iSearch: Psychology

link   A reference to a location on the Web that is embedded in the text of the Web page. Links are usually highlighted with a different color or underlined to make them easily visible.

listserv   Strictly speaking, a computer program that administers electronic mailing lists, but also used to denote such lists or discussion groups, as in "the writer's listserv."

lurker   A passive reader of an Internet *newsgroup* or *listserv*. A lurker reads messages, but does not participate in the discussion by posting or responding to messages.

mailing list   A subject-specific automated email system. Users subscribe and receive email from other users about the subject of the list.

modem   A device for connecting two computers over a telephone line.

newbie   A new user of the Internet.

newsgroup   A discussion forum in which all participants can read all messages and public replies between the participants.

plug-in   A third-party software program that will lend a Web browser (Netscape, Internet Explorer, etc.) additional features.

quoted   Text in an email message or newsgroup posting that has been set off by the use of vertical bars or > characters in the left-hand margin.

search engine   A computer program that will locate Web sites or files based on specified criteria.

secure   A Web page whose contents are encrypted when sending or receiving information.

server   A computer program that moves information on request, such as a Web server that sends pages to your browser.

Smiley   See *emoticon*.

snail mail   Mail sent the old fashioned way: Write a letter, put it in an envelope, stick on a stamp, and drop it in the mailbox.

spam   Spam is to the Internet as unsolicited junk mail is to the postal system.

URL   Uniform Resource Locator: The notation for specifying addresses on the World Wide Web (e.g. http://www.abacon.com or ftp://ftp.abacon.com).

Usenet   The section of the Internet devoted to *newsgroups*.

iSearch: Psychology

Web browser   A program used to navigate and access information on the World Wide Web. Web browsers convert html coding into a display of pictures, sound, and words.

Web page   All the text, graphics, pictures, and so forth, denoted by a single URL beginning with the identifier "http://".

Web site   A collection of World Wide Web pages, usually consisting of a home page and several other linked pages.

iSearch: Psychology